PLANTING CHURCHES IN THE REAL WORLD

Joel Rainey

MISSIONAL PRESS

Published by Missional Press
149 Golden Plover Drive
Smyrna, DE 19977
www.missional-press.com

Printed in the United States of America

ISBN: 10: 0-9798053-2-5
ISBN: 13: 978-0-9798053-2-5

Cover art concept and design by Sam Raynor.

Author's Note

Many of the stories contained within this book are told from memory, and great care has been taken to ensure the accuracy of all accounts. Due to the limitations of memory however, it is possible that the recollection of some events may not be as precise, or in chronological order. For these and any other mistakes, I alone bear the responsibility

Praise for
Planting Churches in the Real World.

———————————

Church planting is not for the easily discouraged. The average
new church is less than 100 attenders after four years, but most
conference speakers and book writers tell stories of hundreds
after the first year-- a reality few church planters experience.
Rainey paints a picture of reality, including both the difficulties
involved in starting a new church, and the evidence that planting
a church is worth enduring those difficulties. If you are a planter
drunk with vision, this will sober you up. But, it is more than that.
It also shows that church plants make a difference whether they
are thousands or dozens after the first year. I've known Joel for
years, and he tells the stories from his own journey-- teaching
lessons he learned the hard way. It's real world church planting
and it is worth your time.
-Dr. Ed Stetzer, author of *Planting Missional Churches*.
Director of Research, Lifeway Christian Resources,
Nashville, TN

"Dr. Rainey amuses the reader with countless stories of life on
the field. His "lessons learned" approach to the book serves as a
clear warning for future church planters: "The Kingdom of
Heaven is near you, but this won't be easy!"
-Dr. Jack Allen, Director, The Day Center for Church Planting.
New Orleans, LA

"Candid, winsome, thoroughly biblical, keenly missional, and sensibly linked to the real world. Don't be fooled. The weightiness of this little book is inversely proportional to its size, and its wise counsel will help point a safe way through the tangle of neglected assumptions, misguided strategies, ill-founded hopes, and unintentional blunders that accosts the unwary planter on the way to church. Well done!"
-B. Spencer Haygood, Senior Pastor, Orange Hill Baptist Church. Marietta, GA

"Born in the ward of real world experience, *Planting Churches in the Real World* is theologically sound, theoretically tenable, and practically accessible. During a time when starting a church can be faddish, Rainey's work is a dose of both Biblical wisdom and common sense that will stop many would-be church planters before a frustrating failure, and direct many others onward toward biblical success."
-Marty Duren, co-author of *Journeys: Transitioning Churches to Relevance.* Lead Pastor, New Bethany Church. Buford, GA

"Reality bites, as the saying goes. Yet in the age of incredible lostness in America, we must see church planting for what it is . . . a way to spread Gospel influence to every, man, woman and child. High birth weight churches, although fun and influential for the Kingdom, are not the norm, nor are they the answer. Joel Rainey has captured the reality and yet the incredible potential of church planting. New churches running less than 100 are key players in the Kingdom. Small does not have to mean ineffective. Small groups of missionary Christians are critical to our mission and our future. Way to go!

-Dr. Dino Senesi. Church Planting Movement Leader, Columbia, SC

TABLE OF CONTENTS

To Amy,

My wife, and partner in the Gospel,

Without whose counsel, skill,

And influence,

I would have never planted a church.

ACKNOWLEDGMENTS

God has graciously brought many people into my life and ministry for whom I am truly thankful. My friends and colleagues have been most helpful as I wrote these pages. In particular, I want to thank Jack Allen, Spencer Haygood, Dino Senesi, and Marty Duren for their editorial input. Through their critique of my writing, these men gave me appropriate "iron-sharpening" corrections and suggestions, without which this book would be nothing more than an inferior attempt at instruction.

In addition, I want to thank David Phillips, my friend and colleague at Missional Press for his encouragement and enthusiasm about this project. What most don't know about David is that he doesn't just run a publishing company. He is also pastor of a small, young church, and has a vision of church multiplication as big as the lost population around him. As a guy literally working in the "real world" of missions, his excitement over this project was but one indication to me that I was on the right track.

My first church planting experience came from my brothers and sisters at Sanctuary Church (formerly True Life Church) in Greenville, South Carolina. Most of the experiences I recount in these pages come directly from my attempts to get this church off the ground. Although few are left at that church that would even recognize me, I will never forget them, nor will I forget the valuable lessons I learned during the four years that these dear people allowed me to be their pastor.

Finally, I want to thank the churches of the Mid-Maryland Baptist Association, who have allowed me to serve them and continue working within my passion to see more churches started. I am convinced that I serve among some of the most skilled and dedicated pastors and church planters in the United States. I am honored to serve them, and offer this book in the hopes that it will contribute to the God-sized tasks to which they have been called.
Soli Deo Gloria!

Joel Rainey
Columbia, Maryland

Introduction

The first responsibility of a leader is to define reality.

-Max DePree

In the interests of full-disclosure, let me preface this book with the following statements. I am not what most would consider a "highly successful" church planter. The stories you read in these pages will likely confirm this fact in your own mind. Truth is, before you finish reading, you may wonder why on earth you picked up a book on church planting written by a guy like me!

When my family and I moved from central Kentucky to South Carolina to plant my first church, it was what church planters call a "cold start," meaning that my family made up the initial congregation, our home made up the total available facilities, and our tithe made up the total church budget. Unlike what you read in many church planting texts, I was unable to gather a strong core of volunteers within 6-9 months. Actually, it took 13 months to build a rather mediocre core of 13 adults. While meeting the minimum personnel needs, this was far from

1

what most who plant churches would define as adequate. We didn't launch with 200, but instead celebrated with 48. At the end of our first year, the time period in which most texts say you should be working on how to break the "100 barrier," our fledgling congregation was still trying to break the "50 barrier." Financially, we were just below "broke."

In addition, I made all sorts of mistakes through the process. I appointed leaders to positions for which they were not ready, spent monies that should have been saved, saved monies that should have been spent, frequently lost both my patience and my temper, spent too much time in administration and not enough with unbelievers, or with my family, and in general wasted a lot of time on things that in the grand scheme, really didn't matter.

In retrospect, I really should be driving a truck for a living!

That church, which was birthed in 2001, has since joined forces with an older congregation, moved to another part of the city, changed its name, and acquired permanent facilities. Its current location is now atop a hill just outside downtown Greenville, South Carolina. The church has about 120 in worship, has assisted in starting two daughter churches, and by God's grace continues to impact its community in a positive way. But it's no Saddleback and it's no Mars Hill.

In other words, I'm the rule, not the exception!

In a 2003 study of new churches, Ed Stetzer discovered that of church planters assessed, the average size of their new

congregations after three years was between 70 and 80 people[1]
In the simplest terms, this means that the average church planting
experience bears little resemblance to the experiences often
written about in books. To be sure, the authors of those books (at
least most of them) are godly men and great leaders from whom
you and I can learn much. I thank God for extraordinary churches
like Saddleback and visionary leaders like Rick Warren. I am
astounded by the innovative approach of Mosaic in Los Angeles,
and the creative leadership of Erwin McManus. The story of
Seattle's Mars Hill Church is indeed a story of God's saving grace
making a huge impact in one of the least churched cities in North
America. Still, the reason we love these extraordinary stories is
because they are, well, extraordinary! Too often when observing
an incredible move of God's Spirit, we think that if we somehow
just figure out the pattern, the strategy, the paradigm, we can re-
create what it took God Himself to create.

Knowing that God can indeed move in powerful ways
wherever and however He chooses, I pray you and your church
are one of those extraordinary, incredible exceptions. But more
than likely, God will use you and your church planting efforts in a
very "ordinary" way. This means, of course, that your efforts will
be anything but "effortless."

---

[1] Ed Stetzer. 2003. *An Analysis of the Church Planting Process and Other Selected Factors on the Attendance of SBC Church Plants.* Alpharetta, GA: The North American Mission Board.

Perhaps the most helpful and insightful of all statements made of church planting comes from Aubrey Malphurs, who says plainly that "[C]hurch planting is hard work."[2] For the most part, those who plant churches will discover that they have entered an occupation that requires lots of physical, spiritual and emotional sweat. And the majority of these will find that all in the end, all their efforts amount to a very "ordinary" church.

My own calling and experience in church planting was indeed ordinary. Unfortunately, prior to my planting experience I had read too many extraordinary stories of rapid response by potential core members, unexpected surges in growth, airplanes full of people coming to Jesus . . .you get the idea. As a result of having my head in the clouds and feet planted firmly in mid-air, I came to see my experiences as less than acceptable early on. I felt that there was no way I could have a lasting impact on my community unless I could boast a burgeoning congregation. Basically, I defined "success" in the same way as the authors of the books I was reading, without thinking through how such success would look in my own context.

The fact is that if you are located in suburban Wichita, you simply cannot judge success by the same standards as those who plant churches in downtown Los Angeles. If you are seeking to reach goths in small-town America, and have the same expectations as a guy trying to reach Baby Boomers in suburban

---

[2] Aubrey Malphurs. *Planting Growing Churches for the 21st Century.* Grand Rapids: Baker Book House, 1998.

4

Chicago, you will likely be sorely disappointed. And if you forget that the success stories of North Point, Saddleback, Willow Creek and Mosaic represent less than 1 percent of new churches, you will see them as the norm rather than the exceptional move of God that all of them represent.

In short, to have the right expectations, you need to plant your church in the "real world." The aim of this book is to introduce you to the real world of church planting so that your feet will remain on the ground while doing the work. This book is also written so that when the challenges come and you are wondering whether this new baby you are trying to birth will ever breathe its first breath, you will know that you are but one of an enormous number of your brothers who face these same issues almost every time a church is planted.

And if indeed your church ends up being the rule rather than the exception; remember that God uses the seemingly mundane and ordinary to accomplish great things. When searching for a nation out of which to bring the Messiah, He chose the small, insignificant nation of Israel. When looking for a deliverer for His people out of Egypt, He chose a stuttering murderer named Moses. When making a call on a "point man" Apostle, He chose a vulgar, redneck, indecisive hot-head named Peter. And today, when searching for someone to plant the next culturally relevant, Gospel-centered, city-reaching church, He chooses, for the most part, ordinary guys like you and me.

Even in the real world, God does great things! Let's spend the next few pages talking about some principles that can lead to seeing those great things happen.

-1-

Why You Do What You Do

My calling to church planting began to take shape while serving as pastor of an established church in Kentucky. I served a church that was located in a small town of around 1500 people. On the surface, it was the epitome of "Mayberry," and Amy and I loved our time there. Overall, our experiences were good and the people were wonderful to us. Over the course of my ministry with them, God doubled the size of our average worship attendance, with 60% of that growth being from people who came to faith in Jesus. Honestly, we could have stayed there for the rest of our ministry. But there were a few things that troubled me about my work there. For one, a good percentage of our town was African American, and more than 60% of this town's population was below the poverty line. Yet with the exception of a couple of families, our church overwhelmingly consisted of white, middle class folk. While we enjoyed healthy growth, that growth was coming from the outlying areas of our town, not the town itself. Basically, this meant that in spite of our growth, we really weren't making much of an impact on our immediate area.

My concerns were further exacerbated while reading a book by Robert Lewis. This pastor of a 3000-plus member church had chronicled their journey to becoming a church that had a genuine impact on its city. But this journey began with the realization that their church, regardless of its enormous size, was a failure because it was not influencing its immediate context with the Gospel.[3] Through this book I came to realize that a church is only a success to the degree that it is able to impact its community in a positive way. If they wouldn't miss you if you disappeared, then you probably have no reason to exist.

At the height of this personal struggle, I received a visit from an African-American Church of God pastor, who came into my office to introduce himself, and inform me that he was in our town to start a new church. The more of his vision he shared with me, the more excited I became about the potential. Subsequently, he and I visited a few homes together, and I introduced him to the Mayor, Chief of Police, and Postmaster, all of whom worked on exactly the same piece of real estate in our small town. In the middle of our experience together, it occurred to me that my burden for the poor of the town was about to be lifted by this man of God. Though he ultimately decided to plant his church to the

---

[3] Robert Lewis. 2001. *The Church of Irresistible Influence.* Grand Rapids: Zondervan Publishing House.

south of our town, I realized that largely due to his race, background, and method of ministry, he was very effective in reaching many of those people I had been impotent to reach!

This was the point at which I began to realize the truth that it takes all kinds of churches to reach all kinds of people. Simultaneously, God was renewing a burden in my heart for the area where I grew up. Prior to the 1990s, upstate South Carolina was known for agriculture and textiles, and the churches that ministered to this area rightly accommodated that agrarian culture. But as the economic and cultural landscape began to shift, and the work force relocated from cotton mills to automobile manufacturing plants, established churches, on the whole, had great difficulty adjusting to this shift. Further research led me to discover that more than 70% of churches in my home state were either on a plateau or declining, while the unchurched population in this central area of the "Bible Belt" had surged to more than 60%.

Lying in bed one night, I asked my wife to pray with me about the possibility of moving back to South Carolina, and starting a church. Over time, she was not only supportive, but more aggressive about the necessity for new churches than I am. Her first response, however, was to sit straight up in bed and ask me if I had lost my mind. "Don't you know there is a church on every corner down there?" Such a response from my own wife should have been sufficient warning of the objections that would later come.

As much as we hate to admit it, there are times when things other than our calling hold us to our current ministry assignment. As a pastor, there were a few frustrating weeks when I just wanted to throw in the towel, but that would have required re-locating the family and looking for another job. When faced with the choice between the two, family security won out! I know you aren't supposed to say things like that, but any pastor who has been in ministry for more than a couple of years knows exactly what I am talking about. Most just won't say it publicly.

But when planting a church, all of that changes. You will likely face merciless days that will make you wonder whether the only reason you got into this in the first place was a missed dose of Zoloft® on one of your "good" days. One day in particular seems to stand out in my case. A couple that had been excited about our new church and had all but begged me to join our core group suddenly wouldn't even return my phone calls. After weeks of hearing about their excitement at our innovative approach to ministry, I received a short e-mail from the wife telling me that they had, from the start, been uneasy about the contemporary nature of our church, and that they were returning to a more traditional setting. Along with their presence and partnership in ministry went their tithe, which at this time in our core development phase equaled about 20% of our total inside giving.

On that same day I received a visit from the local fire marshal. Through the sheer providence of God we had received the opportunity to rent a fantastic facility for pennies on the dollar, which was a good thing given our current financial status. The fire marshal's visit was to inspect that facility. If you have had any experience at all with fire marshals, you probably know how this story ends.

Before his visit was over, I was informed that since the facility had not been in use for several months, it would need to be "upfitted" and brought into compliance with all current fire codes. Furthermore, since the facility purpose was to change from a day care center to a church, I had to file a "change of use" petition to our county government. This process would initiate additional county-required upgrades to the facility, which in turn would require the services of an architect. Finally, after thousands of dollars (which we didn't have) had been spent, we would be ready for the fire marshal to return and make his inspection. What all of this meant was that a facility we thought we could occupy in a few weeks would now take much longer, cost money we did not have, and likely delay our launch date, which had already been heavily advertised.

In that moment I felt as though someone had taken a sledge hammer and crushed our future with it. In less than a day, I went from feeling great about how we were progressing, to wondering how we would continue. When you face moments like that as a church planter, it's hard not to give up. At this point, there was very little money to continue, no other staff to help, and now (at least for the foreseeable future) there was no building. In moments like this, only one thing will keep you focused: God's call!

Elements of a Biblical Calling

Aubrey Malphurs states that God "hard wires" each of us prior to birth with the skills and talents required to fulfill our divine purpose. This "divine design," he says, "includes such things as our temperaments, and our natural gifts, talents, and abilities. When we accept Christ, God adds other things as well, including our spiritual gifts. All of this constitutes our divine design of makeup, our special "wiring" or "chemistry."[4]

Such insight allows us to see that God's call is not only real and necessary, it is also discernable. Sometimes it is difficult to work through discovering God's purpose for oneself, largely because those who have grown up within the church, as a whole, have an almost existential view of what we have simply entitled "the call." When I was a child, that phrase was used in only two ways: to describe the call of God to either the pastorate, or the mission field, and for years there has existed in some circles the unchallenged assumption that a calling to ministry is neither tangibly observed nor measurable in any way.

To be sure, if God has called you to plant a church, it began with what the Apostle Paul referred to as a strong aspiration for the office,[5] and such internal aspiration is totally subjective. In the end, you and only you know for sure whether

---

[4] Malphurs. 1998, 80.
[5] 1 Timothy 3:1

12

God has called you to this task. At the same time, there are other elements of a Biblical call that are often overlooked.

The Biblical Qualifications to Fulfill Your Calling: Assuming you will also be the pastor of this church, it is imperative that you examine yourself, and allow others to examine you, in light of the Scriptural qualifications for the office as recorded in 1 Timothy 3:1-7 and Titus 1:5-9. Much more will be said about this in Chapter Three.

Gifts Commensurate with the Perceived Calling: Conversation alone can be very convincing. This is why the most successful business scams are done over the internet. Anyone of average intelligence, if given the time, could talk a good game about almost anything.

For example, I'm fairly certain that in an internet chat room, I could convince you of my calling to play basketball for the NBA. In fact, if all I had to do to play professional basketball was convince a coach of my passion for the game, I'm quite sure I'd be sporting a jersey within days. But one sight of my two-inch vertical jump would put to bed any notion that God wired me to take on Yao Ming on a basketball court. In short, if God has called you to a task, it makes sense to believe He has also equipped you to perform that task.

If you believe God has called you to plant a church, part of the way such a call is confirmed is to see whether God has given you abilities, natural and spiritual, commensurate with what is needed to get a church off the ground. As a general rule, church planters need to be gifted to some extent in the areas of leadership, administration, evangelism and hospitality. Being weak in one of these areas doesn't necessarily negate the validity of your call. But given the task of a church planter, it is safe to say that if you can't inspire and organize people, or if you don't already spend time with lost people, then either God hasn't gifted you in these areas, or you are being disobedient by not utilizing the gifts He has given you. Either way, your chances of successfully starting a church that will reach people for Jesus are slim.

The Affirmation of God's People Regarding Your Call: God's church is no less than a divine invention of genius for several reasons. At least one of those reasons is that through the church, you have an avenue by which your gifts and calling can be observed, honed, and developed. Maybe you think you are a good preacher, when in reality you can't form a coherent sentence! While it is important for you to personally examine your perceived calling in light of the gifts you believe God has given you, it is equally important that your brothers and sisters in your local church have the opportunity to speak into your life regarding these same issues.

Obviously, this means that before you think about starting your own church, you should already be actively involved in an existing one. While I'll discuss bad reasons for starting a church later, for now I'll tell you that if you don't currently love the church enough to give yourself to it in covenantal relationship, you have absolutely no business trying to start one and ask others to do what you yourself are not willing to do. Don't ask people for financial support for a new church if you aren't currently giving from your own pocketbook. Don't ask people to join a core group that will require ample time-sacrifice if you currently aren't even showing up for worship. God's people need each other, and if you are going to plant a church, you need God's people to affirm that calling and support you in it.

In addition to the advice and counsel of your church family, you should seek counsel from other brothers and sisters by participating in a church planting assessment. Though lengthy and tiring, church planter assessments, if done correctly, give you a thorough look into how God has prepared you. They also give you a strong sense of whether God has indeed built you to start a church. Current research[6] has demonstrated that potential planters who submit to an assessment prior to starting their church are twice as likely to succeed, and most supporting agencies now require assessment before funding is made available for planting a church.

Be careful, however, to ensure that you are assessed by people who know what they are doing, and who will love you enough to be brutally honest with you. In Maryland, our denomination has a highly effective assessment process.[7] Other church planting networks also have effective assessment

---

[6] Glenn Smith. 2007. *Improving the Health and Survivability of New Churches: State of Church Planting USA.* Leadership Network. [database online]; available from www.leadnet.org; Internet; Accessed 26 October, 2007.
[7] For more information, see www.bcmd.org or www.startchurches.com.

processes, and should be considered on the basis of the area where you feel God wants you to plant. For example, if you are considering a church plant in an urban area, the ACTS29 Network has a success rate of more than 99%, and most of their church plants are located in urban areas.[8] Most networks like ACTS29 also work with multiple denominations, meaning that you can network with folks who know what they are doing, while at the same time remaining true to your own denominational heritage.

In the real world of church planting, calling isn't just important; it is crucial, and it is central. Without certainty in this area, the difficulties involved in starting a church will likely be overwhelming. With this in mind, the most important thing you can do before you plant, is to be sure God has called you to do it!

Wrong Reasons to Start a Church

I hear these reasons all the time, and they come from a variety of different people. I've talked with young people and old people, city people and country people, and I've discovered that God has gifted people from every walk of life to plant churches. I've also discovered that people from every walk of life can get the idea of starting a church based on all sorts of wrong-headed reasoning. So before we talk about the Biblical reasons behind a genuine calling to start a church, let's look at three of the most prominent "bone-headed" reasons to do so.

"I'm tired of doing church the same old way." I also call this the "cutting-edge rationale" for starting a church. Usually, it

---

[8] See www.acts29network.org

16

comes from someone in a traditional church who tried to take it in a more contemporary direction and nearly lost their head for it. They have seen those on what we call the cutting edge of ministry, and want to lead a church that will put them there as well.

The trouble however, with the cutting edge, is that it is sharp! Not a few have fallen off, and even more have been severely wounded by that proverbial "edge." The simple fact is that the cutting edge isn't all its cracked up to be!

Remember parachute pants and mullets? At one time, both of these were on the cutting edge of fashion. As I write this paragraph, it is the day after Halloween. At our church's youth party this year, my wife unpacked some old clothes from the 80s, "boofed up" her hair, and as a result had one of the hit costumes of the night. The point is that what was in style less than two decades ago is now used to make a hilarious Halloween costume! Eventually, all things innovative end up in an antique store, or on the rack at Goodwill®.

Mark Driscoll offers a strong warning to those who would presume to build a church on innovation alone:

> *Equally damaging to reformission is the tendency, most common among young Christians frustrated with the constraints and failures of backward-looking churches and ministries, to ignore church history and its lessons in pursuit of unrestrained and undiscerning innovation. The irony of this innovation is that churches and ministries that pursue it become so relevant to the culture that they are, in fact, irrelevant and are unable to call lost people from or to anything*

17

*because they have lost the distinctive and
countercultural nature of the Gospel. Unrestrained
and undiscerning innovation not only contextualizes
the Gospel to fit a culture but also capitulates it to a
culture.*[9]

To be sure, I sympathize with any pastor whose
congregation refuses to recognize the shift from a print culture to
an image culture, and subsequently refuses to add multi-media to
their worship. At the same time, when you plant a church, do it
acknowledging the likelihood that in 20 years, something will
replace the data projector as well. Therefore, if you want to start
something that will last, its core value better be something deeper
than the desire to be cutting edge. Gadgets and fads, like the
grass and flowers of Isaiah, will fade away. Only the Gospel is
forever.

"I'm angry at my deacons." I call this the "I want to do it my
way" rationale for church planting. As an ordained Baptist pastor,
I have experienced deacons meetings that were, shall we say,
less than amicable. That being the case, I understand the
frustrations that come when lay leadership are stubborn, inflexible,
and unwilling to do what is necessary to move the church forward.
But starting a church isn't the answer to this dilemma, primarily
because I have found that often, I can be just as stubborn,
inflexible, and unwilling as the most obstinate deacon I have ever
met! In short, doing it your way will be, in the end, just as

---

[9] Mark Driscoll. 2004. *The Radical Reformission: Reaching out Without Selling
Out.* Grand Rapids: Zondervan, 52.

18

ineffective as doing it their way. The problem isn't that they aren't following you. The problem is that they aren't following Jesus. Similarly, if you go out on your own simply because they aren't doing it "your way," chances are you won't be following Him either! **"I'm going to be the next Rick Warren."** OK, so no one has actually ever said this to me. Nevertheless, most guys who set out to start a church are convinced that they will be the next church planting "Rock Star." I won't spend much time dealing with this issue here, because the entire book is actually for the purpose of addressing this. For now, suffice it to say that if you are in this for you, do everyone else a favor and quit now. God has assured us that He will share His glory with no one. Scriptural principles like that one should be enough to warn us of the dangers of attempting to build a church on personality.

The Right Reasons to Start a Church

If God has genuinely called you to plant a church, He has not only given you the gifts and skills necessary to make it happen, but also a passion guided by Biblical reasons why it *must* happen. Others have written more eloquently than I on the Christological, Ecclesiological, and Missiological reasons to plant, and I will not attempt to improve on their work here. What I will speak to is how these reasons should be personally appropriated to your own calling.

The Christological Reason: Everything begins and ends with Jesus and His Gospel. The center and circumference of your church planting conviction should be no less than a realization that

19

Jesus is not yet worshipped as He deserves to be, and a determination to do something about that!

The Ecclesiological Reason: Jesus did not simply leave it to us to decide how best to fulfill His commands. He ordained that His work be accomplished through the local church. Churches should be planted because, as Mark Dever has so eloquently stated, the church "is the God-ordained means his Spirit uses to proclaim the saving Gospel, to illustrate the Gospel, and to confirm the Gospel. The church, then, is the conduit through which the benefits of Christ's death normally come."[10]

The Missiological Reason: As you explore your calling to this task, one crucial element of that calling will be not only the conviction that a Gospel-centered church be planted, but that it be planted in a particular place, among a particular people. Like the Apostle Paul, who was forbidden to enter Asia and Bithynia and the very next day led directly to Macedonia, God has a place and people among whom He desires this church be planted.

Planting a church is one of the toughest things you will ever attempt, even with the call of God. With this in view, it is probably wise to affirm your calling so that you aren't doing it without Him. If you are convinced of why you are doing this, such a genuine call will serve as an immoveable anchor in Satan's strongest hurricane!

---

[10] Mark Dever, "The Church" in *A Theology for the Church*. Daniel L. Akin, ed. Nashville: Broadman and Holman, 2007, 812.

-2-

Building a Team

One of the first mental steps in planting a church (aside from a psychiatric report officially declaring you insane) is to realize that you can't do it alone. If your vision is to become reality, you need what Malphurs refers to as "a well-mobilized lay army."[11] To have this, you not only need the right number of people, but also the right kind of people. The trouble is that gathering and mobilizing such people is much easier to read about than accomplish.

Think for a moment about what you are asking people to do. The job description isn't necessarily the sort that attracts the kind of "top notch" people you want. Basically, you are asking people to commit a lot of hours, money, and energy to something that doesn't yet exist.

---

[11] Malphurs, 1998, 150.

In exchange for their commitment, they get no pay, little recognition, and relationships that, in the beginning, are erratic and unpredictable. Truth is, they could get all of that in an established church. At least in that environment they would have a building in which to worship, and somewhere to send their kids. Even unbelievers who have rarely attended church have a hard time getting their arms around the purpose for all of this work. Once you see all of this from the perspective of those whom you are asking to work with you, your expectations become more realistic. The problem is most planters, at this stage, usually think more about their own perspective than they do that of potential team members.

Once Amy and I decided to pursue our calling to plant a church, I immediately began calling old acquaintances and friends, asking them to pray with me about the possibility. Prior to our stint in Kentucky, we had ministered in a couple of different churches in my home state. As we were departing for seminary in Kentucky, several of our friends in these churches told me explicitly; "If you ever come back to this area as a pastor, I will join your church."

Boy, did those statements ever feed the ego!

Remembering those tacit commitments, I contacted many of the people who were close to us in our former ministry there and talked with them about our calling to plant. In December before our move to the area, I even managed to get several of them to attend a "vision meeting." About 25 adults showed up for

22

an hour of discussion fueled by a passionate presentation I gave on the state of the area, the decline of established churches, and my vision for a fresh approach to ministry that would make a significant impact. Keep in mind, these were people who were dear to our hearts. They all loved us. They had all prayed for us. In fact, many of them had financially supported us during seminary, and almost every one of them had said they would allow me to be their pastor should I ever move back.

Of the 25 or so who showed up, exactly none joined us. In fairness to them, they weren't being dishonest. Instead, they expected that I would return and serve as pastor an "established" church--one with a building for their comfort and a nursery for their children. Since my vision initially offered none of those things, they decided to stay where they were. In other words, they weren't dishonest, and they weren't uncommitted. They were simply uninformed about my intentions. Once they got the information, it didn't fit their understanding of ministry, and they in due course responded by turning me down, which sent me back to "square one" with regard to building a team.

Subsequently, when we finally arrived on the field in August of 2001, the adults in the core group consisted of my wife, my brother and me. A few weeks after our move, one other guy joined us as well. To add to this number, I began doing neighborhood surveys every Saturday morning in various communities around the area. Two weeks and approximately 100 homes later, we hosted our first Bible study meeting in our home.

Amy prepared a great spread on our dining room table, enough food for at least 20 people. The appointed time came and went. Finally, about 15 minutes later, my brother and the other guy showed up. A few minutes after this, we heard a knock at the door.

A husband and wife who lived right behind us on an adjacent street decided to respond to my invitation, and brought their three children with them, which more than doubled our attendance! Beating the streets and meeting all those people had resulted in six adults at our first Bible study. We had what I thought was a great time of fellowship and discussion. The kids played well together, and the couple seemed highly engaged and interested in our discussion. I was so effective and compelling in casting my vision that night—so eloquent, winsome and persuasive--that this couple never returned. The next week, we were back to four!

Experiences like this are painful, and can create a lot of anxiety and questions regarding your motives, your approach to ministry, and even your calling. This is especially true if you spend too much time prior to your plant reading stories of fast-growing core groups. In the real world, most churches get started in a much less spectacular way!

Building a Great Team

After completing more than 50 graduate school studies of Fortune 500 companies, Les Carter and Jim Underwood discovered a stark dichotomy between the "public face" of many companies and the perceptions held by the companies' employees. The study revealed that of these companies, "almost all had major deficiencies in the leadership area. In many cases, those same firms' annual reports tout the company's attitude of 'empowerment' toward their employees. Yet, when we had the opportunity to talk with some of those employees, empowerment was the last word they thought of in trying to describe how they were treated."[12]

In the midst of all the negative perception, Carter and Underwood found one very bright spot, at Southwest Airlines: "Of all of the companies we dealt with . . .they really are committed to 'walking the talk.'"[13] Their point is that building a great team means fulfilling the expectations of team members, which means that the leader's first task is to uncover those expectations, and determine whether or not they can be met. Frankly, as a church planter, there is no possible way for you to meet everyone's expectations, which means that you may have to bid farewell to many who indicate an early interest in what you are doing. In the long run, this will be a good thing, as the first members of your team will determine the eventual makeup of the entire church, and you don't want people who will, intentionally or unintentionally, distort the end picture. Others may play a more peripheral role in what you are doing, while still others will make up the heart of your

---

[12] Les Carter and Jim Underwood. 1998. *The Significance Principle: The Secret Behind High Performance People and Organizations.* Nashville: Broadman and Holman Publishers, 1.
[13] Carter and Underwood. 1998, 3.

core group. What follows are a few principles to guide you as you seek to build a great team.

A Great Team includes more than the members of your church. Believe it or not, the majority of those on your team won't be members of your church. But some of these people will prove to be your most vital team members, even if they never set foot into one of your worship services. Chief among this number are those you enlist to regularly and passionately pray for your church planting efforts. My friend Jack Allen, who teaches church planting at a seminary in New Orleans, suggests that in light of the nature of your work, you should enlist between 300 and 500 people to pray for your efforts. Among these will be a smaller number who receive specific requests for prayer, and then an even smaller number whom you can trust to pray about the intensely personal matters that will occur during your church planting experience.

The need for prayer is much greater than you may think. If church planting is anywhere nearly as effective as Peter Wagner says it is,[14] then surely Satan must hate it more than anything else you and I could attempt in order to reach lost people. From experience I can testify that the enemy will come after you. He will come after your family. He will also come after the families in your core group. I'll speak more about this in later chapters. Still, in

---

[14] Wagner, who teaches at Fuller Theological Seminary, has been widely quoted referring to church planting as "the single most effective evangelistic methodology under heaven."

26

the face of such warfare, prayer is the only hope you have. Pray alone. Pray with your family. Pray with the team you are building. Enlist as many serious prayer-warriors as possible to fight with you in this realm!

In addition to prayer-team members, you will likely also have those who are not members of your church, but support you financially. Our initial core was made up largely of college students and young singles, with only a couple of more mature families. By the time of our launch date, our tithes and offerings added up to a whopping $300 per week! (Most of our original core members were college students, and 10% of textbook returns and stale pepperoni pizza doesn't add up to very much.) In that kind of financial environment, you will initially need more than just the inside giving to underwrite everything that needs to be done.

Aside from a denominational salary subsidy for me, the outside support we received consisted of cash, as well as nursery equipment, computer equipment, and sound equipment. These needs were met mostly by individuals who had absolutely no desire or calling to join our church, but who nonetheless saw the value of what we were trying to do, and wanted to help us get it done. Just remember that when planting a church, "team member" doesn't necessarily mean "church member."

My experiences have taught me to warn potential church planters not to be surprised by who doesn't join them. Early in our efforts, there were people whom I thought for sure I could count on to be part of our new church who never caught our vision, and subsequently, never joined. Nevertheless, of all the people who meet this description, I can't think of one who didn't readily agree to lift us up in prayer, and not a few supported us financially at different points along our journey as well.

One of the people who occasionally supported us was my dad. You don't get any more "establishment" than my dad. He likes pews, hymnbooks, and big, wooden pulpits. In spite of all these preferences, he chose to join me on a trip to visit a new downtown church with whom we were seeking to work. Being a man of few words, he said nothing throughout the entire visit. Thinking back, I'm sure he was working hard to process the whole experience. The age of the average attendee at the church was 19, and several rode on skateboards into the coffee shop where this church had set up worship. Wild hair and even wilder clothes dominated the room, as did the tattoos sported on various body parts. A few sat on chairs around tables, a few on couches in the back, and many sat on floor pillows in the center of the room while listening to the pastor's message. That message, spoken in a very atypical context for a church in the south, was the Gospel of Jesus Christ. As we left the service, and got back into the car, I wondered what my father's reaction would be. I was surprised, after being raised in the home of a man who shed very few tears, to see my dad getting emotional. "I could never be comfortable in a place like that," he said, "but to see all those young people coming to hear about Jesus . . .something good is happening in that place." My father has never planted a church, and will likely

28

never serve in anyone's core group. But his exposure to that experience left him a life-long proponent of starting new churches.

There are a select few out there who will be part of your core team. There are many more like my dad, who will likely never worship and tithe regularly at your church, but who believe wholeheartedly in what you are doing. Give these people an avenue of partnership with you. You will both be stronger for it.

A Great Team is Held Together by a Gospel Vision. Of course, by "held together" I don't mean to imply that all who make up your original team will display an indefinite, unqualified allegiance to you and the church you plant. "Turnover" on a church planting team is to be expected. When your initial core group is assembled take a good long look. Chances are less than 10% of them will still be around twelve months from that point. As I write these words, the church I planted just finished celebrating its 6th birthday. Of those who helped us start the church, only one family was still present for that celebration, and that family will soon be moving to another state, where the husband will begin serving as pastor of another church. In an environment that contains the kind of flux necessary to plant a church, turnover is inevitable.

At the same time, something needs to serve as a source of cohesion to keep the team focused on the mission while they are with you. The buzz word for this "something" is what we call "vision," and without it, the new church is doomed before it even gets off the ground. But "vision" isn't what most think it is. Over the years, I have seen this term used to describe some existential and over-romanticized notions that are anything but God-given. So when we talk about vision, let's be sure we know what we're talking about.

In what is possibly the best book written on the subject matter to date, Andy Stanley rightly contends that a genuine vision will carry with it something that will "feel like a moral imperative," because it ultimately "will be in line with what God is up to in the world."[15] Such a vision, he goes on to say, "is enough to cause them [your team] to jump in."[16] In short, if the vision is Gospel-centered, genuine, and subsequently compelling enough to attract and retain the kind of people needed to plant a church, it will be based on something bigger than you.

Much can be learned from the business literature regarding how to grow your church. Indeed, when we search for guys to plant churches, some of the best come equipped already with entrepreneurial skills that were honed and developed in the business world. At the same time, planting a church is not, in the end, about growing a great and successful organization with qualified staff and a healthy bottom-line. Church planting, in the end, isn't about growing a church. It is about transforming a community. And the only vision powerful enough to accomplish this is one that is empowered by Gospel conviction, and defined by Gospel truth.

---

[15] Andy Stanley. *Visioneering: God's Blueprint for Developing and Maintaining Personal Vision.* Sisters, OR: Multnomah Press, 1999. 25.
[16] Ibid., 129.

Such is exactly the reason why some contemporary attempts to minimize the atoning death of Jesus, or the reality of eternal judgment, are so dangerous to a new church. While other resources are available that more thoroughly and effectively deal with these issues, I feel compelled to issue a brief warning here about the dangers of re-defining the Gospel. For example, one popular proponent of changing the message as well as methods answered the question "who goes to heaven" a few years ago in this way:

> *Why do you consider me qualified to make this pronouncement? Isn't this God's business? Isn't it clear that I do not believe this is the right question for a missional Christian to ask?*[17]

Such internal "conversations" about the Gospel that end with the kind of ambiguity referenced above will distract your people from actually proclaiming the Gospel. Conversations that don't produce genuine followers of Jesus are ultimately fruitless, and at worst heretically dangerous. The vision you cast for your people must include strong convictions concerning Biblical authority, and a sound doctrine of Jesus and salvation. Foolish conversations that debate things like the reality of heaven and hell only result in more people entering the latter location.

This is not to say that there cannot be a variety of theological opinion within your church. Driscoll refers to the

---

[17] Brian D. McLaren. *A Generous Orthodoxy*. Grand Rapids: Zondervan, 2004. 112.

categories of "open handed" and "closed handed" issues as a way of distinguishing between what is doctrinally debatable, and what is absolute. In our church, we had elders who were Calvinists, and those who were not. Among our leadership there were differences of interpretation on the nature of the so-called "sign gifts." And when we talked about the second coming of Jesus, the viewpoints espoused represented a broad cross-section of those described in the theology texts.

Nevertheless, by the time you are assembling your team, the "closed-handed" issues should be settled, and one of those settled issues should be the nature of the Gospel. The church is the instrument of God's redemption in the world. For it to be what God wants it to be, it must be certain of what people are redeemed from, by whom they are redeemed, and how they are redeemed. If this message is clearly proclaimed within the context of a compelling picture of how the Gospel will transform the community in which you are planting, such a vision will provide a cohesion that will hold your team together during the really tough times that will certainly come.

A Great Team is Encouraged by its Leader's Commitment. It was not one of my better moments. Our launch team decided to co-sponsor an outreach event with the local recreation department. More than 500 people would eventually show up to play on inflatable rides, eat free ice cream, line up for a free chiropractic screening, get their faces painted, play with balloon animals, be entertained by clowns and M&M characters, and

32

register to win some really nice prizes. Problem was, it was less than an hour before the event was to start, and I was the only one there! My frustration and anger was obvious to the first members of our team who arrived. In retrospect, I know that my frustrations were wrongly aimed at my team. After all, they were no more than 30 minutes late arriving at the event, which in core group phase is the equivalent of being punctual! Deep down, I wasn't frustrated because they were late, but rather, because I was alone. Before my church planting journey was over, I would experience many more such moments.

At some point, every church planter will face the reality that it really is "lonely at the top." You will come to the realization that no one is more committed to this new church than you. Hopefully, in that same moment you will also realize that this is as it should be.

Most of the existing church planting literature extols the virtue of a guy's visionary capacity. More than any other behavioral characteristic, the ability to cast a compelling vision of the future is a non-negotiable skill, without which the church will never be planted. But once the action starts, there is another behavioral characteristic that is just as important. We call this characteristic "resilience." Basically, all the vision in the world is worthless without the doggedness and determination to see it realized.

In my experiences with planting churches, this is the most problematic area I have seen with regard to why churches don't make it. Your team will be inspired to join by your ability to cast vision. But they will only stay on board in proportion to the dedication they see in you. That's why I say give me a guy who lacks a bit in casting vision, but won't quit, over a guy who can talk about the future but doesn't have the boldness to move over, around, and through all the barriers in order to move toward that future.

The bottom line is that the dedication of your people will never exceed your own. If you don't have what it takes to finish the job, neither will they. Conversely, if your team sees you consistently facing and overcoming difficulty, they will start to think you really believe in what you are doing, which in turn will encourage them to stick with you. Their commitment will never be as great as yours. But if yours is what it should be, a lower level of that commitment will be replicated in a dedicated church planting team.

A Great Team is Perpetuated by an Outward Focus. As you build your initial core, you will discover many people whose main focus will be something other than making disciples and transforming the community. Usually, these people will reveal themselves with statements like "give us a call when you get a building," or "as soon as you guys start that worship service, I'm on board!" But occasionally, folks like this will find their way into your core development process. When they do, your leadership and direction must be strong enough, either to change their perception, or send them packing. Otherwise, you will have a team, but it won't be a great one.

Our church saw many such people come and go. While there were several observations that allowed us to identify these folks, there were two predominant foci that immediately revealed their true intent. The first of these was the "what will you do for me?" attitude. These were people who were willing to consider joining our team, but first wanted to know what they would get in return for their commitment. They wanted to know specifically; "How will your church serve me?" A good response to this question that re-directs the focus outward is to turn that question back on the person asking it. Try responding with "How will you use the gifts and abilities God has given you to serve the community through this church?" Another way to answer this question is to simply say "We will serve you by empowering and equipping you to make a difference in your sphere of influence with the Gospel." Those who don't get it will usually leave shortly after this. Those who are challenged and inspired by such a statement will likely make great team members.

The second most predominant focus involved people who were always talking about how it was in their last church. My strongest run-in with this attitude occurred while we were teaching our core about our understanding of church government. A few of our folks, like me, had been raised Baptist, and as such had been exposed for most of their lives to a deacon-led, democratic model of congregationalism that more closely resembled the US

Congress than the Biblical picture of church leadership. As I began to forward a more elder-led model of congregationalism in our church, a few objections arose. None of these objections had a Biblical rationale, mind you. Instead, the typical response was "I've been in church my whole life, and we never did it this way."

Objections like this will be made in regard to your style of worship, your budgeting process, your evangelism strategy, and even how you encourage fellowship. Such objectors must be told clearly that this is not their previous church, nor will it ever be. New churches cannot thrive in the past. Their success is predicated on their future focus.

The best church planting teams are those that can keep their focus on what really matters: namely, the conversion of souls, the changing of lives, and the multiplication of Kingdom influence. As such, your recruiting efforts must include a description of success that is no longer defined in the traditional terms of building and congregational size, or budget health. Success must be defined by Biblically faithful ministry that results in community transformation. When such is seen as the "end game" of your church planting effort, the natural result will be that you will gather people who are defaulted toward an outward focus.

The Balance of a Great Church Planting Team

Some who plant churches will tell you that when building a team, you should focus exclusively on the unchurched. Others by contrast will contend that without a team stacked with growing, mature believers, you will be doomed to a spiritually immature and

36

struggling church. Actually, "balance" is a good word to remember when assembling your initial team. Obviously, you want your growth to come primarily from the world, and not from other churches. At the same time, you should build your team with the understanding that, like your community, it should consist of people who are at various points along their spiritual journey. **You need mature Christians.** One of the overblown myths of core development is that you should only target lost people. Reality demands that you have at least a proportional number of people on your team who have followed Jesus for a very long time. Of course, part of my understanding of "mature" is that in addition to their cognitive knowledge of the Bible, they also possess a spiritual passion that motivates them to impact their sphere of influence for Christ in a positive way. If a guy has exhaustive Bible knowledge and years of experience in "church life," but has no significant relationships with people outside the church and no desire to see his community changed by the power of the Gospel, then his knowledge and experience has all been wasted on himself. Such attitudes and behaviors are unlikely to change, and such people should be passed over when seeking to build a team.

Still, as you are developing your initial team, be sensitive to the spiritually mature people who are open to what you are doing. Eventually, you will need elders, deacons, small group leaders, and others to come alongside you and help move the church forward. Such people will likely be needed long before growing Christians on your team will be ready and qualified to assume such responsibility.

You need young Christians. The greatest advantage of this group is that most still have connections with their lost friends. Most are excited about their new faith, and most are eager to connect their passion with their lost friends. In addition, this group will help refine the church in a way that will make it more evangelistically effective. While more will be said about this group in a later chapter, for now I'll say that as you think through the best way to build team in your area, your overall strategy must include a way to effectively disciple this group of people.

You need lost people. Obviously, this group will not make up the "membership" of your church—at least not until they turn to Christ and publicly confess Him by baptism. Nevertheless, you want your people to be consistently engaged with people who don't know Jesus, and one of the best ways to ensure all of them get this experience is to bring those people into the church, and in some cases, even take them on mission with you.

In our experience, we discovered that lost people came to Christ more quickly if they were given clear avenues of participation in church life. In short, many people are attracted to the church community *before* they are converted to Christ. That said, you will need to determine how involved you will allow unbelievers to become in the life of your church. While they cannot be members of your church prior to conversion, there must be a way for non-members to "test the waters" via their

38

involvement. Among these activities should be a clear list of things in which you will allow lost people to participate. Can they participate in mission trips? Can they play instruments during worship services? Study the Scriptures and draw your own, Biblically-informed conclusions about such issues. But regardless of what you can and cannot allow, be sure there are ways for unbelieving friends to engage and be involved in the life of the church before they come to Christ.

From the very beginning, you want your church to be a place where those yet to know Christ will feel at home, and will sense the freedom to be themselves, ask hard questions, and explore the Christian faith in a safe place. If lost people are a part of your "outer core," this goal will be much easier to attain.

Having others planting with you is important, because you can't do it alone. Having the right people planting with you is also important, because the wrong people will set the church on wrong course—a course that will most likely be permanent. But most importantly, having the right people planting with you is important, because this is the group out of which will come future congregational leadership. It is to that critical issue that we now turn.

-3-

Leaders and Leadership

Two experiences began my exploration into how churches should be led. One was my experience growing up in a church with a strong congregational conviction that was fleshed out by purely democratic processes. Though I continue to have a great appreciation for the church where I grew up, I noticed that little to nothing could be substantively accomplished in this church without numerous committee meetings, motions, amendments, and secret ballots. I remember wondering how many more might be won to Christ if business was simply turned over to trusted leaders and missions became the primary concern of all those who showed up to cast their votes.

The second experience involved the church where I assumed my first staff role. It was not a church of the same denomination as the one in which I was raised, and my responsibilities as an interim staff member were temporary. Still, during that six month assignment, I saw the consequences of too much centralized power. Quite the contrast to the church in which I grew up, this church allowed for almost no input from the laity. Ruled by one pastor, the congregation simply bowed to his wishes, and dissenters were quickly shown the door.

At some point between these two extremes, I figured there had to be an approach that appropriately balanced the accountability every church leader should have toward his congregation with the respect and trust every congregation should give its leaders. Of course, at this point in my life and ministry, the sum total of my reading on the issue of church leadership was pretty much confined to my denomination's confessional statement, meaning that at the time, I was the least-qualified person on the planet to critique how churches were governed. Still, I knew enough to know that something just didn't seem right about the way many churches are led.

That said, let me emphasize that I continue to work with churches that are governed in a variety of ways. In the years I have been in ministry, I have seen just about every leadership paradigm that can be utilized in the church, and the truth is both that they all work, and they all fail. The key to leadership is often not so much the structure as it is the leader himself.

Nevertheless, as a church planter, it is imperative that as you are building the core of the church that you look for those in that core who will be the leaders with you in this new church. And if they are to lead, they need clear instructions as to *how* they will lead, which means you have to decide how you believe God wants this church to be governed.

In a new church, this issue is too important to simply leave it to tradition, or ignore it altogether. Steven Cowan rightly laments the way in which decisions are made in churches without first forming biblical and theological understandings of how the church should arrive at these decisions. There is, he contends, "a familiar and traditional way that individual churches (and denominations) conduct their polity, but there is little or no theological reflection on that tradition. Things are done a certain way because that's the way they have always been done."[18]

Among the more than 25 churches I have personally been involved in seeing planted, a plethora of leadership paradigms exists. The most successful of these church plants varied in terms of their approach to church leadership, but in every one of them, the planter thought long and hard about the Biblical teaching on the subject, and how that teaching would impact and influence his context. This is, I believe, a key ingredient to a successfully governed church. James Emery White correctly observes that "a church's structure is crucial when it comes to rethinking the church because it is a church's structure that supports and facilitates the purposes and mission of a church."[19]

---

[18] Steven B. Cowan, ed. 2004. *Who Runs the Church? 4 Views on Church Government*. Grand Rapids: Zondervan, 7.
[19] James Emery White. 1997. *Rethinking the Church: A Challenge to Creative Redesign in an Age of Transition*. Grand Rapids: Baker Book House, 94.

Another key ingredient is ensuring that those who take the reigns of leadership are qualified by their calling, lifestyle, and ability to do the job. Furthermore, those called and qualified have to work well together, and they have to trust each other. Who cares if the structure is right if those who fill the positions in that structure aren't qualified to be there, or if there is suspicion and dissension among those who lead? So, while I'd love to convince every reader to share my own studied opinions as to how a church should be governed, this chapter will focus on what I believe to be a far more important matter; selecting and developing the right people to lead.

Selecting Qualified Leaders

Larry Osborne has observed that when searching for leadership, most churches simply look for a warm body and a willing heart. His contention is that "anyone who faithfully supports the church and works hard eventually finds himself or herself rewarded with a seat on the board. While I know of no church that claims this as their method of selection, I know of plenty where it is, in fact, the way things are done."[20]

But dedication and willingness, while admirable, are not sufficient. It cannot be stressed enough that when looking for those who will stand beside you in senior leadership, you hold each candidate up against the light of passages such as 1 Timothy 3, Titus 1, and 1 Peter 5. While my purpose here isn't to provide a

---

[20] Larry Osborne. 2006. *The Unity Factor: Developing a Healthy Church Leadership Team.* Vista, CA: Owl's Nest, 39.

thorough exegetical analysis of these texts, there are five general characteristics described in all three of these texts that are important to look for in a leader.

He is a mature man. The New Testament is explicit in its warning against appointing someone who is young in the faith (1 Timothy 3:6). In addition, all the other character quality passages presume that he has been a believer long enough for people to observe his character.

In the first stages of church planting, you will be tempted to place men in positions of leadership before they are ready. I gave in to that temptation on a couple of occasions and can tell you from experience; this is not a mistake you want to make! Obviously, an immature leader hurts the church, because the congregation, for the most part, will never rise to a level of maturity that exceeds its leadership.

But placing someone in leadership prematurely hurts that person as well. Because I placed people without sufficiently testing them, I was responsible for their failure, and the subsequent personal pain they incurred. Admittedly, the process of discerning a person's spiritual maturity is a delicate task, and you won't always get it right. Nevertheless, it is incumbent on you as the planter to do everything you can to ensure that the people you place in leadership are actually ready to play at that level. Although the Scriptures do not prescribe a definite "time limit," concerning how long one should be a believer before being considered, I would be very cautious in appointing people young in their faith to any position of leadership.

He is a disciplined man. In other words, he can control himself. He is disciplined in the areas of his temper, his prayer and Bible study, and his appetites. Remember that the primary function of church leadership is to facilitate the making of disciples whose minds and hearts are transformed by the sanctifying power of the Holy Spirit. Such a task is very difficult when the church leader himself is, for example, a hot-head, a glutton, or a pervert.

As you survey the people around you and prayerfully discern who God desires to lead, be careful to watch closely the lives of those you are considering. Are they prone to allow their temper to get out of control during moments of high stress? When the pressure is on, do they run to Jesus, or to a liquor bottle? When it comes to the alcohol issue, there are Christians who think a pastor shouldn't drink at all, and others who think it's OK. But neither group is given room by Scripture to wink at drunkenness, or a lifestyle of dependency on strong drink. The same is true, by the way, of food. Maybe you don't run to the liquor bottle for comfort in stressful moments. Maybe instead you run to the refrigerator.

I gained an enormous amount of weight during my first pastorate, largely because of a lack of discipline. Thanks to an apnea diagnosis and a loving wife who wanted her husband to have a long, healthy life, I was able to lose 47 pounds and get back to a healthy weight. I am confident that if I'd had a problem with alcohol, I would not have been approved for ordination. It troubles me however, that my weight was never an issue. Similar comments could be made about sexual addictions, prescription drug addictions, anger management issues, and patience. All of these are ultimately issues of self control, which Paul tells us in Galatians 5:23 is one of the fruits of a mature believer produced by the Holy Spirit. As you prayerfully select church leadership, be sure that their lifestyles, and your own, embody self-discipline.

He is a family man. Early in my ministry, I was rather flippant about the issue of whether a single man could serve in senior leadership in a church. While I have yet to become a "legalist" in this area, I am now much more cautious about appointing a single man. This is not because I think singleness automatically disqualifies a person from leadership. (In that case, neither Jesus nor Paul would be fit to serve.) Yet the Pastoral Epistles are explicit in stating that a man proves his fitness to lead in the church chiefly and primarily by the way he leads his own home.

For the most part, this means that senior leadership in the church will be comprised mostly of "family men," who through their families have shown themselves to be sexually, mentally, and emotionally faithful to their wives, admired by their wives and children, and good managers of their homes. Personally, I would never appoint a man to leadership without first having a long conversation with the wife and kids. If a man can't command the respect of his own children, how on earth will a congregation of adults ever follow him? And if the wife doesn't admire her husband, such will be clearly seen, and eventually replicated, by other families in the church.

I was once asked to consult with a church that was plagued by a great number of broken families. I know the divorce rate is high for churches in general. This church, believe it or not, boasted a rate of broken marriages that made most other churches look like the picture of marital health and bliss. As I dug deeper, I discovered that among the leadership there was an abnormal amount of marital discord. One very influential leader eventually confessed to me that he and his wife hated each other, and only remained married for the sake of convenience. It should surprise no one that the families of that church were a mirror image of the family life among the leadership. Take a good, long look at the family life of any potential leader. How he leads his family will be exactly how he will lead the church.

He is a Sociable Man. In short, this means that people inside and outside the church have to like the guy. Inside, a leader should be "respectable." Basically, this means that others look at his life and want to replicate it. When they observe his self-control, parenting skills, the way he romances his wife, how he responds to and manage conflict, and how he handles Scripture, they should say "I need to follow his example."

Outside the church, leaders should be a valued part of their community. Even if a man has all his doctrinal "ducks" in a row, if he is a total jerk to his neighbors and co-workers, this is not a guy you want representing your church. Talk to his neighbors.

48

Talk to his co-workers. Talk to the parents where his children attend school. If he represents Christ as a church leader should, most people outside the church will say "his beliefs are a little weird, and I'm not sure I buy into all that 'Jesus' stuff, but he is a good neighbor, and our community would be less without him." An organization's leaders make up its face, and when it comes to the church, you want that face to be one that speaks the truth with a smile.

He is a Bible man. Aside from the ability to manage his home, Scripture dictates only one other skill a senior leader should possess; the ability to teach the Bible. While many today would contend on the basis of this that a senior leader be a "preacher," there are many other ways to effectively teach the Bible. Conversely, he may be a very eloquent speaker who has very little knowledge of the content of Scripture, even if he is a seminary graduate. I know it's tough to fathom, but trust me on this. I've been to seminary, and graduated alongside a few guys whose actual understanding of the Scriptures was woefully lacking.

This qualification also doesn't necessitate that every pastor/elder be a professional theologian. They don't necessarily need to know Hebrew and Greek, or be an expert in Systematic Theology. Nevertheless, leaders must be able to give direction to the body of Christ, and that direction must be based on God's Word, meaning that they need a basic understanding of the Old and New Testaments and their relationship to each other, skill in interpreting the Scriptures, ability to practically apply the text, and the ability to demonstrate how every part of the text points sinners to Jesus.

All of this is to say that those in leadership must have knowledge of the Bible, and a personal love for it. Such men will prove their skill in this area primarily in the way they disciple their families. When the wife has a question about the Bible, or needs personal spiritual direction, who does she approach first? If it's her pastor and not her husband, then there may be an issue with the husband's ability to effectively disciple his wife. Are his children learning the Bible from him? Does his family view him as the spiritual authority? These are important questions to ask, because the best prediction of what kind of pastor/elder a man will be is to see what kind of husband and father he already is.

Once men are selected, I think it is wise to provide continuing education for them, so that they continue to grow in their knowledge of the Word. This doesn't necessarily mean sending them to Bible College, although some may desire this. Two of the guys on our elder team were enrolled in the local Baptist University by the time I left the church. But most of our guys learned the Bible through a weekly meeting we held at the church. We studied Old and New Testaments, Systematic Theology, Biblical interpretation, and explored various ways to reach our lost friends with the Gospel. If you have genuine "Bible men" on your leadership team, they will cherish these times of cohort learning.

Does he have to be a man?

The observant reader has discovered by this point that I am a staunch advocate of male pastoral leadership in the local church. This does not mean that women have no significant place of service. In fact, our church employed women as teachers, small group leaders, overseers of social hospitality, and a host of other ministry roles. Still, I believe the New Testament is clear that those who presume to fulfill a pastoral/elder role must be men.

In the first place, male leadership in the church follows the leadership order that Scripture prescribes for the home. The pastoral epistles are crystal clear that the government of the church is based off of the government God established in the home, with the husband as the head who sacrificially loves his wife and children, provides for them, and takes responsibility for the well-being of all who are a part of his family.

Secondly, male leadership in the church frees the women to fulfill their God-given roles. 1 Timothy 2:11 encourages women to "receive instruction" and thereby be knowledgeable of the Scriptures; an appropriate encouragement given that Paul later establishes a discipleship paradigm in which young women turn to older, seasoned, and theologically-inclined women for instruction.[21] Practically speaking, there will be issues of concern for women that will be inappropriate for a man to address.

---

[21] 1 Timothy 5:1-2

For example, my wife shared with me during our church planting experience how shocked she was at the number of women who had been sexually abused, raped, or otherwise mistreated. There is simply no way for these kinds of situations to be appropriately and adequately addressed by a man. Godly, Biblically literate, compassionate women must be available for such needs. If they are functioning in roles God intended a man to fill, they will not be free to fulfill needed roles such as these.

Finally, male pastoral leadership places the burden for the success or failure of the church in the right place. Just as men are ultimately responsible for the physical, spiritual and emotional condition of their homes, so are they also responsible for the overall health and growth of God's church. God's purpose for women was that they work alongside men as helpers, but He never intended for the ladies to bear the burden of pastoral leadership. And this home and church order finds its origins in creation.

Everyone knows, for example, that it was Eve who first disobeyed God in the Garden. Yet have you ever noticed that in every text after Genesis 3 the fall is blamed, not on Eve, but Adam? The fall took place, not only because of an act of disobedience, but also because the spiritual authority in the home decided to take a vacation from his responsibilities. From the beginning, God intended men to lead and women to help us lead better. We find ourselves in our current sinful mess at least partially because a man refused to assert the leadership God had granted him, confront the serpent, and protect his family.

David Murrow, who is himself ambivalent on this issue, nonetheless admits that the steep decline in mainline denominations is due largely to the dearth of real men in pastoral leadership positions. Recent statistics, he contends, "indicate that denominations that have opened their doors widest to female leadership are generally declining in membership . . .while 60 percent of churches with a male senior pastor suffer a gender gap, 80 percent of congregations with a female senior pastor do."[22]

I cannot stress enough the need to take your time when seeking qualified leaders who will give direction to the church alongside you. From experience, I can testify that placing people too quickly will damage their Christian walk, inhibit the growth of the church, and raise questions about your ability to find the right people. God willing, you will avoid some of my early mistakes in this regard, and for the most part, time and observation are your two best friends in this area.

Ideally, qualified leaders have earned the trust of the people they will lead before they assume a leadership role. James Emery White correctly observes that "good people do not need laws to tell them to act responsibly, while bad people will always find a way around law . . .It takes trust for this structure to

---

[22] David Murrow. 2005. *Why Men Hate Going to Church.* USA: Thomas Nelson Publishers, 155-156.

operate."[23] Unfortunately, the way many churches select leaders, especially pastoral leaders, makes this process of developing trust almost impossible.

Think for a moment about the way most pastor search committees operate. They look for adequate education and training, church leadership experience, a "track record" of growth, and eloquent speaking ability. While there is nothing wrong with a church desiring these qualities in their pastor, the New Testament sets up other qualifications as far more important; qualifications that are often never observed before appointing a pastor. Make sure when you are assessing people for leadership that you don't make this mistake. Look closely at the things Scripture holds up as most important, especially when appointing elder leadership in a new church. Something this young and small won't be able to survive the possible negative consequences of ignoring Paul's warning against laying hands on someone too hastily.[24]

Build Unity Among Your Leaders

So you have searched carefully, taken your time, and God has rewarded your patience and care with Godly men who love their families, love their Bibles, love you, and love their church and want to see it grow. But if you think all of the above is all you need to ward off unnecessary conflict, you should think again!

Our elders all loved Jesus. They were all good men. We all shared the same doctrinal confession, and we all had a

---

[23] White, 1997, 103.
[24] 1 Timothy 5:22

54

genuine desire to see lives changed and the community transformed by the Gospel. In spite of all this, we fought with each other over how much focus to give international missions, who would be responsible for which areas of the church, and even how we would take up the weekly offering. Sometimes the debate was healthy, and served to do some necessary, mutual iron-sharpening. Other times however, we wrangled with each other over things that later turned out to be totally unnecessary. For the most part, this was due to the fact that I was not proactive early in our experience in building unity among the leadership. Thank God for His grace, and my leadership for their patience with me as I figured out "on the job" how to facilitate unity.

I learned the hard way that early in the orientation process, prospective elders need to be told what we will and won't fight over. Doctrinal unity was a "no-brainer" for me. After all, I had not long graduated from seminary before starting this church, and knew there must be a strong doctrinal basis on which we could all agree. What I didn't yet know was that among leadership, there were so many other things that could be fought over.

For example, how did our doctrinal statement coincide with and empower our philosophy of ministry? How did these inform the vision we were seeking to fulfill? And how did our vision, doctrine, and ministry philosophy combined help determine our core values? These were not questions I had even thought about; at least, not until the fighting started!

This reality underscores the importance of clear core values. Of course, part of the trouble with developing clear values is that there is no uniform way to define a "value." Malphurs, for example, defines the values of a church as the "biblical, core beliefs that drive its ministry."[25] Rick Warren contends that values serve to keep the central purpose of the church in focus.[26] In a context of potential conflict, I prefer to think of core values in much more practical terms. Core values define clearly what you will, and won't fight over.

Among our leadership, we made conscious decisions not to fight. We refused, for example, to fight about Reformed theology, although our elders were both Calvinists and non-Calvinists. We also refused to fight over personal preferences, whether they related to worship, community, social justice, or missions. We might find disagreement on these issues that resulted in a need to talk through them and hammer out details. But no one "planted a flag in the ground" over something that was not a clearly defined core value. If they tried, they were stopped. If they couldn't be stopped, they would have been asked to leave. Unity is too important, especially among those leading the church, to allow its disruption by secondary issues.

On the other hand, our values also helped us set agendas based on what was important conversation. For example, one of

---

[25] Malphurs, 1998, 253.
[26] Rick Warren. 1995. *The Purpose-Driven Church: Growth Without Compromising your Message and Mission.* Grand Rapids: Zondervan, 90-92.
56

our values was "acceptance," meaning that our belief that every human being is created in God's image informed how we welcomed people different from us into the church. It informed how we dealt with drug addicts, homosexuals, and others who, in the church environment in the south, didn't always feel welcomed. Another of our values was "accountability," meaning that this God-given image was reason to hold people accountable for their sins. In the end, this meant if a small group leader began to teach that homosexuality was OK (yes, this actually happened), we confronted him. If by contrast someone began cracking "gay jokes" in a way that was offensive to the homosexuals who occasionally attended our church as visitors, we would deal with this as well.

All of this is to say that church leadership should know at the outset what the doctrinal, visional, philosophical and practical "non-negotiable" issues are. If you are united on these issues, it makes unity much easier to attain. But maintaining unity also requires building trust.

Building Trust Among your Leaders

Unity is largely produced by trust. Even those on opposite sides of an issue will find a way to unite if, in the end, they are each able to give the other the benefit of the doubt. And the best way to build trust is to spend time together.

When Amy and I were first married, our biggest fights were over money. Though our philosophies of spending, debt, and stewardship were almost identical, we simply had never applied said joint philosophy in real world situations. I had my money, and she had hers. When we were married, everything became "ours." But since neither of us had ever spent "our" money, the first year of our marriage was spent learning how this was done, and building trust in each other in the process.

In short, the more time you spend with someone trustworthy, the more you naturally trust them. When building a pastoral leadership team, trust comes over time, meaning the more time you can get these guys spending with you and each other, the more rapidly trust will be built.

My friend Andre Rogers is pastor of The Open Door in Columbia, South Carolina, an eight-year old church that has grown significantly over the past four years. Early in our relationship, I asked Andre how he picked the right leaders in his church. "It's pretty simple," he replied. "If I don't like you, and don't like hanging out with you, I'm not going to hire you." When he said this, I honestly thought his answer was shallow, self-serving, and possibly even a bit childish. But in the six years since having that conversation, I have come to see that Andre was on to something!

I can't genuinely trust someone if I don't have a meaningful relationship with them, and I can't have a relationship unless I am investing time in it. As you build a team of leaders, be sure you spend plenty of time together. For starters, make sure you are praying together. Too many leadership meetings simply use prayer to "baptize" conversation that could otherwise take place in any corporate boardroom. God's church has a right to expect its leaders to be men who spend time on their knees together, and nothing builds trust and admiration quite like the humility required to cry out to God in front of other men.

Also, take retreats together. Early in our church planting efforts, I didn't think this was financially possible, mostly because of my perception of a "retreat." On one occasion, I became exasperated while reading about two pastors who described lying on a Caribbean beach together talking church strategy, and sharing this information with me as if I could afford to just hop on a plane and take my leaders with me.[27]

But a retreat doesn't require a tropical environment (although granted, palm trees and a mild breeze from the Gulf can't hurt!). At least once per year, our leadership and their families traveled somewhere together. One year it was to a church plant on the other side of the state to get ideas and brainstorm with their staff. One year we went to our denomination's local camp and conference center, took our own food, and spent the weekend together. One year we traveled together to Gatlinburg Tennessee. Some of the time at these retreats was spent in prayer, some in planning, and some in spiritual formation. Most of it was just spent hanging out with each other. In a couple of cases, the church could afford to cover the

---

[27] See Andy Stanley and Ed. Young. 2002. *Can We Do That? 24 Innovative Practices that will Change the Way you do Church.* USA: Howard Publishing. Just don't read it if you are a church planter. Unless you have a six-figure budget and a core group of at least 150 people, this book will seriously depress you!

total bill for all of us. In other cases, we had to pay some of our own way. But our leadership came to look forward to the annual retreat, and we always left loving and trusting each other a little more.

Another way to build trust is to carry everybody along at the same pace. I learned a valuable lesson early on from Eddie Cox, pastor of Marathon Community Church.[28] As a result of seeing how this church developed leaders, we patterned our own leadership development philosophy after theirs. The theme was simple: "Everybody starts at the bottom." We made it very hard, for example, to access the stage. Let's face it: there are plenty of folks out there who aren't as interested in serving Jesus as they are in being the next "rock star." So unless you had been in our church for several months, you didn't preach, you didn't lead a small group, and you didn't sing. In fact, you didn't even get up to make an announcement! To be sure, we had ways in which you could serve from the first day, but none of these ways came with a spotlight.

With the notable exception of musicians in the band, everyone who came into our church "started at the bottom." It didn't matter what position you held or what great things you may have accomplished in your last church. I distinctly remember confronting a man who had served his previous church as

---

[28] See www.marathonchurch.org

chairman of deacons and chairman of trustees. He let me know in no uncertain terms that he knew how to run a church, and wanted to help us do it better. My response was to literally hand him a toilet brush and say "Thanks for coming, and since you offered to help, our restrooms will need to be cleaned after everyone leaves."

For some strange reason, he never came back!

Leaders of the caliber you need won't flinch at the challenge to serve, in whatever capacity is needed. Just remember what I said in the last chapter about people never rising above the leadership level of their pastor. Michael Anthony observes that "in essence, leaders who can say with humility 'follow my example' will face fewer team fractures."[29] You too have to be willing to "start at the bottom." Once during a clean-up day I had to light a fire under the rear of a less-than-motivated staff member, who expressed his resentment in response, along with his belief that he should not have to be subjected to such base labor. I shared in response that there was still paint under my fingernails from the time we were getting the building prepared for launch, and if I could do it, he could do it.

Finally, you and your leadership need to learn together. Since beginning in the ministry, I've always had a love of books, and in the beginning of our church plant, I was always giving books away. Sometimes these books were actually read. Other

---

[29] Michael Anthony. 1997. *The Effective Church Board.* Eugene, OR: Wipf and Stock Publishers, 128.

times they were simply put on a shelf, and before the second year of the plant, there just wasn't much continuity among our leaders in regard to what they were reading. Until very late in the game, seldom were the times that we were reading anything together. That was a mistake!

Learn together, do life together, and learn to trust each other through the process. Such unity will eventually be replicated among the wider congregation, and when that happens, your church will be ready to change the world!

Clarifying Leadership Roles

Most importantly, the other leaders need to be clear on your role. In the absence of clarity regarding who the "point man" is, another will step into the place that belongs to you, particularly if your team is made up of strong leaders. As the planter, you are the initiating leader. You set the direction of the church, under the leadership of the Holy Spirit.

This doesn't mean that you aren't accountable, nor does it minimize the contribution of the other pastoral leaders. The pattern of the New Testament makes clear that when important decisions were made, they were declared by the leadership as a whole. Still, there was always a "point man" who spoke for the elders, as their functional leader. Whether it was James in Jerusalem or Peter at Antioch, when a big decision had to be made, or a crisis overcome, the church knew who to turn to. And since most likely you will be the only full-time guy at the church (at least at first), you are, by default, the natural person to take the reins. Larry Osborne states that by virtue of time and training, the senior pastor is the best qualified to lead the leaders. "To lead," he says, "a person needs to know the organization inside out— how the parts fit together and how each will be affected by proposed changes." Additionally, the pastor has "a decided advantage when it comes to training . . .when a church faces a tough situation or golden opportunity, the pastor is the one most likely to have been exposed to a similar situation. If not, he'll usually know where to find out what the experts recommend."[30] As you develop leaders, be sure the roles and relationships of each are well-defined and understood, starting with your own. Core development, systems design, conflict management, and every other crucial factor in a new church will be doomed to failure without the right people to lead the effort. With this in mind, this is likely the most crucially important chapter in the book. If a God-called, Biblically-qualified, unified and dedicated team of leaders is at the helm, the "key systems" we will talk about next will be managed with ease. But most importantly, godly leaders will produce a godly church, which will produce a godly community that will transform the world for the sake of godliness.

---

[30] Osborne. 2006, 67.

-4-

Systems, Structures and Simplicity

There is a closet in my study at our home that contains a giant chart. That chart contains a very sophisticated system of attraction, retention, and assimilation that I designed for our new church during our earliest days. Every so often I pull out that chart and think of how much effort I put into making sure every area of ministry was covered by the system I put in place. I had spent too many years trying to correct anemic evangelism and stop the hemorrhaging of individuals out the infamous back door of established churches. At the time, I really thought the answer to these issues lay in finding the right process, and implementing the right attraction and assimilation systems. And mine was quite impressive!

Eight years after all that work, I still occasionally pull out that chart, just to have a good laugh. In the end, our church became almost exactly what I envisioned, but the process of getting us there looked very different from what I originally had anticipated. As I speak with guys who have planted churches, I find that this is a very common experience. As they moved through the process of getting their churches off the ground they discovered, as I did, that sometimes it just doesn't happen the way you think it will. In fact, the most impressive churches I know of seem to have the most unsophisticated structures.

That is not to say that structure is unimportant. On the contrary, the success of your outreach strategy, small groups, worship, and assimilation plans are predicated largely on the viability of the church structure you build. In addition, whether all of the above work to create synergy or inertia depends on how your ministry processes have defined the relationship of all the different ministries to each other. That said, the structure of your church is a central and essential part of making disciples.

The Essentials

While each church is different, there are certain structural realities that are common to all of them that must be in place prior to beginning public worship. Simply put, while many of the structural issues will be dealt with as you are building the church (sort of like assembling an airplane while it is in flight), there are a few key systems that, generally speaking, have to be in place even before you get started.

Musical Worship: This one is almost a no-brainer. Ideally, within your initial core team there should be someone God has gifted musically and called to lead that aspect of your worship. Sometimes, you are even blessed with several folks who play instruments, and who sound good together. Reality however, demands that you admit something from the outset; gifted, God-called, volunteer music leaders are the proverbial "needle in a haystack," and it is imperative that anyone who shares the stage with you be *both* called to the task, and gifted for the task. Whether you utilize non-Christians as musicians is a matter of conscience, but those who *lead* worship should be strong followers of Jesus, or you are headed for trouble!

Early in the life of our church, we secured a few good musicians for which we were very thankful. But six months after our launch, I discovered that one of our musicians, who claimed to be a Christ-follower, was sleeping with his girlfriend. I, along with another elder, counseled with him to no avail. He saw nothing wrong with his current living arrangement, and was offended that we even brought it up, so I had to remove him. It was a very difficult time for me, not only because we lost a talented musician, but because of his refusal to turn and subsequent anger toward me, I also lost a friend.

Before the end of that year, God had sent us three others to replace the one who left, but the interim period was hard. The lesson I took away from that experience was that talent divorced from godliness and a genuine calling adversely affects worship.

At the same time, godliness without talent also adversely affects worship. Early in my ministry, I didn't feel this way, primarily because I was taught that in a church environment talent doesn't matter, as long as a person wants to bring glory to God.

"If they are singing to the Lord," one of my mentors used to say, "it doesn't matter whether they have talent." This may be true, but if you have no talent for singing, it is possible that even the Lord doesn't want you on stage in front of people who will fail to see how God gets any glory out of that noise!

I know it sounds horrible to say, but if you think about it, it also makes sense. Why would we ever encourage anyone to function in any area where they were clearly not gifted? This is especially true when it comes to music. When seeking leaders in this area, don't be afraid to play the part of crotchety American Idol® judge Simon Cowell.

So what if there isn't anyone in your core team qualified to assume this responsibility? Well, you have a hard decision to make. Thankfully, modern technology allows for the use of worship DVDs and other tools that will allow a congregation to get along OK without a music leader, and that scenario is certainly better than having the wrong person lead. But regardless of how you decide to proceed, you need to know in advance how the worship component of your church will be facilitated.

Finances: There is an old saying in ministry: The two things a pastor should never touch are the secretary, and the money! Its crude, I know, but not nearly as crude and dishonoring to God as are the stories of men who wrecked their ministries by violating one or both of these unwritten rules!

You can get several opinions from authors more knowledgeable than me regarding what is and is not appropriate.

Personally, I think it is OK, especially in the early stages of a church plant, for the planter to make unilateral spending decisions. However, there has to be accountability. Neither you nor your spouse should be the bookkeeper, or the holder of the checkbook. God willing, there will be someone on your core team who can assume this responsibility. Just make sure they know what they are doing. Better to "farm out" the financial work that to leave it to someone on the inside who is inept.

If there is no one on your team who can do this, I suggest finding another church whose office staff will agree to handle the money for you. If you have a sponsor church that is assuming the responsibility for getting you started, you might ask for their assistance in this area. For the first year, we had the advantage of a sister church whose office staff graciously agreed to process donations, keep our books, and most importantly, send me my support check! There are a variety of ways this issue can be appropriately handled. The important thing is that you don't handle it on your own. Before your church goes public, make sure baseline financial policies are in place, and qualified people are administering the books. In addition, you should secure an outside advisory team of pastors and mature believers who will talk honestly with you about your needs and set your salary until the church has inside leaders who are able to take over these responsibilities.

Childcare: Unless you are predominantly reaching out to retiree communities, or planting a house church, this component will be essential. A key thing to remember regarding childcare in a new church is this: Have as much of it as is necessary, but as little as possible. During the first four weeks of our public worship, a sister church agreed to supply childcare workers for us that would allow all children through the fifth grade to attend a children's church while their parents worshipped with the adults. Aside from the fact that this approach conflicted with our philosophy of family worship, the real issue came one month into our public worship services when those volunteers went back to their church, leaving us with huge vacancies to fill. A hardworking young lady volunteered to run the entire childcare program for us, but after a few months, totally burned out, and she and her husband left the church. To a large extent, this was due to my negligence toward that young couple, and allowing them to "burn the candle at both ends" in order to keep a comprehensive childcare ministry running.

In addition, unless God directly calls her to do it, your wife should not be the person running this ministry. If she starts doing it, she will always be doing it. As a mom, Amy took her turn doing childcare, but had she taken this ministry over simply because "no one else will do it," she would have burned out herself, as well as possibly cheated someone God did call out of the blessing of working in that area. Remember that you are the church planter, and finding leaders is your responsibility, not hers. Don't burden her with things she is not called to do. Be a man and handle leadership vacancies yourself.

If your church is normal, this will be the most challenging area in which to find leaders. You will have Sundays when no one shows up, so know in advance what your "backup" plan is going to be so that your Sundays are truly about worship, and aren't reduced to being all about childcare.

I share all of this to stress that while children's ministry is an important component in most new churches, it should help enhance and strengthen other ministries in the church, not control them. In the beginning, just having a clean, bright, colorful childcare area for babies and toddlers is sufficient, along with dedicated workers who have been through a thorough criminal background check. Nonetheless, prior to any public services, you should, at a minimum, have the space, personnel, and equipment necessary to minister to small children in their own worship context. When Amy and I visit a church, we don't expect a separate kids program for our 7-year-old. He is old enough and mature enough to worship with Mom and Dad. But if the church has nothing at all for our 2-year-old, we won't be back, and we have been following Christ and active in church life for years. Unbelievers will be even less forgiving if in the beginning you don't think and plan carefully for their children.

Guest Relations: Each church planter has a different title for these people. Some call them "ushers," others "greeters," and still others utilize silly names like "seat shepherd" or "seeker of seekers." Give them whatever name you think appropriate. Be as "cornball" as you want. But make sure guests to your church are given the attention they need.

For one thing, if all goes as it should, you will have many more guests in the early days than you will regular attenders. Personally, I'd aim for a "1 to 5" ratio of regulars to guests. So for example, if you have a core team of 10, you should probably shoot for around 50 people at your first service. Such a ratio will give a challenging, yet healthy and manageable balance to your church.

It has been said that the average first-time guest makes up his or her mind whether to return the next week within a matter of seconds after entering the *parking lot*. While everyone has a responsibility to reach out to new people, it is important to assign specific people who will bear responsibility for doing all they can to ensure that guests to your church will want to return.

As you survey the team God has sent you, make mental notes of the skills and passions that each one possesses. As you cast vision to your team, make sure they stay aware of all of the above-stated needs. When in prayer, ask God to supply the harvest workers needed to fill those essential areas, and then use whomever God sends you.

Designing the Discipleship Process

The reason you are starting a church is because the people coming to you aren't where they need to be, which means that a crucial part of your job is to figure out the most expedient process by which they can become all that God intends. Different churches have different ways of doing this that depend largely on their context and primary focus group. Still, there are some elements common to all church systems that will be true of your church if it is genuinely making disciples.

The Structure has an "end game" in mind. My friend Earl Gray serves on our associational staff as Consultant for Spiritual Formation. I don't envy Earl, primarily because he works within a very diverse area in which our churches utilize just about every discipleship process known to man. For the most part, this is due to the ethnic and cultural diversity of our area, and the accompanying truth that each of these environments calls for a contextualized approach to making disciples. For that reason, Earl may meet with a church that utilizes a traditional Sunday School model, and later in the day meet with another church that utilizes "Life Transformation Groups,"[31] or small groups made up of no more than four people. Still later, he may meet with a cell church pastor. But his first two questions to all are exactly the same: "What does a fully functional follower of Christ look like in this context?" and second, "How will you begin to arrive at this picture?"

These questions reveal an assumption about making disciples. Genuine followers of Jesus, while having many things in common, will arrive at their God-given identity in different ways,

---

[31] For further explanation of LTGs, see Neil Cole, *Cultivating a Life for God: Multiplying Disciples Through Life Transformation Groups.* Carol Stream, IL: ChurchSmart Resources, 1999.

depending on the culture in which they live. For example, in many Hispanic cultures, the "machismo" understanding of manhood is a sinful and horrible distortion of the Scriptural picture of real men. For many in this culture, being a man is about how "macho" you behave, how domineering you are over your family, how many babies you can make, and by how many women you can make them.

By contrast, our church dealt with young men who were simply loser meatheads without jobs, who still lived with their mothers, were lazy, unmotivated, and irresponsible. In both of these cultures, the "end game" is the same; godly, Jesus-loving men who work hard, provide for their families, are faithful to their wives, and shoulder the responsibility of leadership in their homes and churches. The process of getting to this point, however, is largely determined by who you are seeking to disciple, meaning that the process of discipleship in our church was different than what it would have been had we been planting in Central America. **The Structure is consistent with the vision of the church.** In short, the structure of your church should be determined by the vision of the church. Any part of your church structure that is not tied directly to your vision is baggage that will hold you back. This is true even in established church contexts, but even more critical for a new church.

When we began our small group ministry, one of our chief core values was "multiplication." We set a rule that once you start a group, you have a year to multiply and create another group, or
74

we would shut you down. Although we weren't totally inflexible with this, we used this rule when, for example, the same group of four people remained unchanged for 20 months, and demonstrated no desire to grow.

This value was put to a great test when our largest small group failed to live up to this value. One of my elders led this group, and for weeks had been telling me, "I have between 27 and 30 people in my living room every Wednesday night. They are literally sitting on window sills and in the floor, and we have no more room for growth. I keep telling the people its time to start another group, but they refuse to leave." After several weeks of this, he finally called me and said "I'm shutting it down." Sure enough, at the next meeting, he informed all gathered that if they wanted to keep the group going they were welcome, but they could no longer meet at his house because he was starting a new group.

Two families left the church because of this action. But within a month, we had almost 40 people being discipled in two small groups, with a view toward starting a third. I'll admit that shutting down our largest small group was an intimidating prospect. But had we left it intact, we would have been untrue to our identity and vision.

The Structure is contextually appropriate. There were 48 people at our first worship service, and within a month, that number climbed to the mid-50s. I was excited about the growth I was seeing, and wanted to capitalize on it. Unfortunately, I only knew of one way to do so; I started a membership drive! My ministry in an established church in Kentucky among middle-class families with children proved this approach to be very successful. The young, single and/or newly married, culturally jaded crowd we had attracted at this new church however, responded in a very negative way toward my attempts to "assimilate" them. Most of them still viewed "church membership" in the same way as a lodge membership, or membership in a union or political party. When non-institutional people view a church relationship in this way, the first step in bringing them along is not to push membership, but to take your time explaining it. This group didn't want to be members of a club; they wanted to be participants in a movement! Because I misunderstood this, I lost the opportunity to capitalize on our new growth, and by Christmas of that year, attendance had dropped into the 20s.

When it comes to structure, the importance of cultural context cannot be overemphasized. How you go about making disciples, and even the terms you use to describe the process, should be designed in such a way that they communicate expectations clearly. For this to be possible, you have to have a thorough grasp of the people you are seeking to reach, and your structure and process should reflect this understanding with clarity.

The Structure is streamlined. My friend Eric Geiger has co-written a book with Thom Rainer that deals exclusively with this issue. "The process," he states, "is straightforward. It is not confusing; it is easy to grasp. The leaders know it, and the people understand it. The process is intentionally kept simple. It is not lengthened. It does not change every few months . . .the church rejects the multitude of new programs and models offered to it."[32]

As you design the process by which your church will make disciples, keep in mind that the structure is not, in and of itself, the goal. The goal is to make disciples, and the structure is a tool that helps you reach this goal more efficiently. Too many churches treat their structure as if changing it would be the equivalent of heresy. In a new church environment, you have the advantage of not having a precedent in this regard, but beware! It is amazing how quickly tradition sets in, even in a new church.

The Structure is clear and deliberate. To be effective, you can't just know where you want people to go. You also need the ability to help them get there. At our church plant, we envisioned responsible, God-fearing, Jesus-loving men who took wives, had children, provided and protected their families, and led in the process of making disciples of their children. We envisioned young women as valuable helpers and advisors to their husbands, as well as excellent mothers. Furthermore, we wanted men and women who remained single to glorify God with their lives as they made their own valuable contributions to the Kingdom.

But those who came to our church, for the most part, were from broken families. Many of the young men struggled with such

---

[32] Thom S. Rainer and Eric Geiger. *Simple Church: Returning to God's Process for Making Disciples.* Nashville: Broadman and Holman Publishers. 2006, 61.

vices as laziness (some more than others), pornography addictions, homosexual tendencies, lust, and pride. Many of the young women, by contrast, struggled with past sexual sin and/or sexual abuse, guilt, and a lack of standards when it came to choosing men. Many had never seen a real family as Scripture defines it, meaning that the road was going to be long. In that kind of environment, change doesn't come overnight, and clear, deliberate steps are needed to help people move in the spiritual direction God intends.

Regardless of who you are reaching, this principle is important. Andy Stanley, Reggie Joiner, and Lane Jones point out that when a church begins thinking in terms of "steps" rather than "programs," "there is a fundamental difference in your perspective. Now the primary goal is not to meet someone's need, but rather to help someone get where they need to go."[33] Furthermore, a clear and deliberate process specifically outlines "how to help people move to the next stage in their spiritual growth."[34]

For us, being clear and deliberate meant moving the people in our church from where they were to where they were supposed to be . . .one step at a time! A young man who grew up with an absent father and domineering mother, and who is hooked on porn and in general acting like a meathead isn't going to become a godly, Biblically-informed, responsible man in one step.

---

[33] Andy Stanley, Reggie Joiner, and Lane Jones. *7 Practices of Effective Ministry*. Sisters, OR: Multnomah Publishers, 89.
[34] Ibid., 90.

Such a journey requires a process that is clear and deliberate. The same will be true for you, whatever your context. You must meet people where they are, and your process and structure should be intentional enough to slowly move them to become all that Jesus intends.

The Structure is Flexible. Too many people in church life think of discipleship as taking place primarily in a classroom. To be sure, learning, whether on the church campus or in someone's home group, is essential. At the same time, most of the spiritual growth that takes place does so while you are simply living life with the people God has called you to pastor.

My family is far from perfect. In fact, I'll be sharing some of our marital struggles that took place during the planting process in Chapter 7. But by God's grace, we have a great marriage, and I am so very thankful for our family. I was also amazed, and honored, that so many of the people at our church who were single wanted to hang out at our home. Prior to our public launch, we met on Friday evenings at our home. On some nights, the last person would leave around 3 AM. Later on, we were told by a few of the young couples who later married that they watched Amy and me, and enjoyed being able to just come over and learn by our example. Sometimes it scares me to think what they might have learned! Nevertheless, some of the most meaningful discipleship didn't take place in a church classroom, or even in the confines of a small group meeting, but instead by just hanging out.

In addition, a few of the young men joined us in doing everything from paintball, to making improvements on the church facility. We taught them how to service a car, fix a flat tire, and balance a checkbook. Conversely, I also learned a great deal from the people who honored us with their presence in our lives.

If the church structure is so overbearing that you are doing more "church life" together than "real life," it isn't flexible enough to allow the kind of symbiotic life change that God intends take place within the fellowship of brothers and sisters who have given themselves to each other in covenant community.

Some Final Thoughts

As you think hard through how your church can be most effectively structured to reach its community, consider the following questions in light of all that has been mentioned. These questions come from training curriculum provided by the North American Mission Board:

1. What is the relationship of each ministry in the church to the others, and how do they all connect to the vision, mission, and values of the church?
2. What is (or will be) the flow of people into and through these ministries?
3. What are the "entry points" into church life?
4. How will your church intentionally help people connect with others?
5. Is there simplicity and clarity of flow?[35]

---

[35] These questions originally appeared in *Basic Training for Church Planters*. Alpharetta, GA: The North American Mission Board, 1999, 79-80.

Structure is a crucial tool that helps disciples move toward maturity, and helps your church move toward the accomplishment of your mission. Give great thought to the process, because it will be tried and tested repeatedly. In fact, the next two chapters describe some of the challenges that will stretch your system to the max!

-5-

Post-Partum Depression

I will never forget the day our first son was born. We were living just outside Louisville Kentucky where I was serving as pastor of a church, and I remember the drive into the city as a time that was exciting, exhilarating, and full of anxiety. For four years prior to this moment, Amy and I had asked God for a child, as well as the circumstances in which Amy could stay home and raise our child. After years of getting ourselves in a position to be a "one-income" family, trying to have a child, and a devastating miscarriage, God was finally answering our prayers in the affirmative.

The first time I saw my son, literally less than a second after he was born, I was in love with him. At this point, I loved my wife enough to die for her, and had possessed this love for many years. But I had spent 14 years developing that kind of love for her. Children are different. No "development" of the relationship is necessary. From the moment I saw him, I would have given my heart, my liver, my kidneys, or any other part of me, and gladly given my own life to save his. Aside from Jesus, Samuel was the greatest gift God had ever given Amy and me at that time. We were elated that God had graciously given us what the Psalmist calls a "gift and heritage of the Lord." We named him after the Old Testament Prophet and judge, so that the etymology of his name would forever remind us that the Lord hears the requests that we ask of Him. A few days later, we took him home, excited about our new life as parents.

And then came the poop and vomit!

New babies are among the most joyous experiences God gives us in life, but let's be real about this; those experiences cost us! Many nights are sleepless. Sometimes the crying is perpetuated to the point that it seems it will never end. Sexual intimacy becomes much more of a challenge. And the diapers . . .oh the diapers!

In order to be good parents, you can't just prepare for the birth. You also have to prepare for everything that comes afterward. If you don't prepare yourself for those monumental challenges that lie ahead, the results will be bad for both you and your new baby. This same principle also holds true when you are "birthing" a church!

Like it or not, if God has called you to plant a church, the issues you will encounter are not at all unlike those of new parents. On a warm September day, a very small group of 13 adults turned into a fledgling congregation of 48 called True Life Church, and a baby was born! Just like any childbirth, once this happens, poop and vomit will follow! That description may be metaphorical, but there will be times as a church planter when you would honestly rather deal with the real thing!

If you want to succeed at bringing this new baby to maturity, you have to know how to care for a baby. But you also need to know how to take care of yourself. While the next chapter will deal with the former issue, this chapter will address what to expect in the days following your public launch, how to be ready for what is coming, and in the process, keep yourself from having the church planters equivalent of post-partum depression.

Some things that are coming

Several new realities present themselves almost immediately after the public launch of a church. The fact that all these realities seem to converge on the planter simultaneously can make life after launch very overwhelming. One of these realities is the numerical reduction of your new congregation. I shared earlier that from September to December, we went from the mid-50s to the mid-20s in average attendance. I also shared that for the most part, this was due to some critical errors on my part. Nevertheless, within a month from your launch date, it is almost a certainty that the dust will settle hard. As a general rule, divide your launch attendance by three, and you will have arrived at the approximate number of regular attendees that will be a part of this new church.

A number of reasons can be given for this phenomenon. First of all, it is likely that you will have a number of "well-wishers" at your first service who have no intention of staying with you, but love you and want to celebrate this day with you. My parents came to our launch service, and made sporadic appearances afterward. But they were very happy in their own church, and were back with their church family the very next week.

Another reason for the coming numerical reduction is that the novelty of a new church tends to wear off rather quickly. The excitement and sense of newness that comes with the first public worship service soon wanes, and those who showed up just to see the fireworks quickly find other things to do on Sunday mornings. The trick in all of this is to be prepared so that emotionally, you don't fall apart or over-react.

A friend of mine started a church, and was anticipating around 100 people or so to show up at the first public service. After telling me he expected to retain about 75 of those people, I told him he had best cut that estimate in half if he wanted a picture of reality. He ignored me, and a month after launch, when the initial crowd of more than 120 had dwindled to around 40, he froze! For six months he was organizationally, strategically, and functionally paralyzed, which in turn only exacerbated the numerical drop that caused his paralysis in the first place. Finally, one of his elders was able to get through to him, and he repented of his leadership anxiety and finally got the church on track.

In retrospect, much of this anxiety could have been avoided had he heeded the multiple warnings sent in his direction regarding the numerical drop that was coming. Possibly the best cure for such anxiety is the kind of long-term thinking that allows you to see the "big picture" of what you are trying to accomplish with more clarity. A friend of mine explained it this way during one of the more trying moments of my church planting experience. He asked me a simple question: "Are you growing a weed, or an oak tree?"

In truth, what fuels a lot of church planting efforts today are gimmicks that focus merely on drawing a crowd and raising lots of money. While such strategies are not sinful in and of themselves, when used merely for the purpose of achieving quick results, they can easily become "weed-growing" tools. Weeds grow quickly, but are easily cut down. Oak trees on the other hand, take much time and effort to grow. But Oak trees have the propensity to survive hurricane-force winds and all kinds of other weather-related catastrophe.

Likewise, when planting a church, be careful to not give too much importance to early growth. Instead, concentrate on building a church that will survive the strongest storms Satan will send its way. Such an effort can't be accomplished with sharp flyers and a slick phone campaign. The discipleship of which I speak is literally done one person at a time, one family at a time.

I have a friend who is pastor of a church in the Atlanta area. Upon assuming his duties there the church had gone through major upheaval, and attendance had shrunk to about one fourth the size the church had enjoyed in its heyday. Further investigation revealed that previous church leadership relied on church growth principles in order to be one of the first "cutting edge" churches in the area with contemporary worship, the use of multi-media, and a seeker-friendly approach to ministry. While there was nothing inherently wrong with this approach, prior leadership pushed these principles alone, devoid of deep and abiding Biblical truth. The short-term result was fast growth. But long-term, the church was unable, due primarily to its spiritual immaturity, to find its way through some heavy controversy, and many people "jumped ship." My friend has led them toward a more Biblically faithful vision that has stabilized the church so that it can begin to make a substantive difference in its community, but the transition has been very difficult, primarily because for years, prior leadership didn't think long-term.

Contrast this with my friend John Mackall, who is pastor of Crosslife Community Church in Elkridge Maryland. John started his church in 2004. Though the church has never seen the kind of accelerated growth witnessed by the aforementioned Atlanta church, John has been careful to ensure that those who enter the doors of his church are adequately discipled. Although his church has never broken the infamous "100 barrier," they have been through some very hard times, and with the exception of a few people, the church has remained intact, largely because of the spiritual maturity among his leadership. In short, John is growing

88

an "oak tree." It will take him much longer, but both he and his church will be stronger for it.

It is true that numbers aren't everything. Still, the chief temptation early in the church planting process is to give too much credence to how many people are showing up. If such is your primary focus, the drop that is most assuredly coming post-launch will paralyze you. Think long-term when it comes to growth.

My Core Group is with me . . .or are they?

Another harsh reality that usually follows on the heels of a public launch is the sudden reduction in the number of committed core group members. Generally, the gradual exit of your core group happens over time. It is likely however, that a few of them will step out the door shortly after the launch. This happens for a number of reasons.

For example, sometimes when you are casting vision, there will be people in the core so excited about the new church that they will hear what they want to hear instead of hearing what you say. For six months prior to our launch, Kelly[36] had been told, along with all of our other core members, that our new church would be led by male pastors. During this time, no one in the core voiced any objections to this theological conviction. But during our first membership class, Kelly absolutely went nuts in front of a whole group of prospective members. She claimed that women would have no voice in our church, accused me of being a male chauvinist, and insinuated that the men we had as leaders in the

---

[36] Name changed in order to protect the guilty.

church were not mature enough to lead because of their age. Needless to say, our first membership class didn't go so well! I visited with Kelly that same day, and confronted her and her husband about her behavior. They came to one more service, and afterward, we never saw them again in our church.

This outburst was a surprise to me, given that I had stressed throughout the core development process our strong belief in male church leadership. My only conclusion as to why such things happen is that when people become a part of your core, sometimes they are so excited about what they like that they don't notice things that to them are objectionable. Simply put, sometimes people hear what they want to hear and block out everything else.

But core members also leave because they develop their own picture of what the church should look like, and when things turn out differently, they feel as though they have been playing for the wrong team. At this point, you have a choice of staying with your vision and bidding them farewell, or acquiescing to theirs and allowing what Malphurs calls "vision hijacking."

I met Dan and Martha[37] through a ministry I was involved in, and they instantly joined our core group, excited about the opportunity to help establish a church from the ground up. Throughout both our private conversations, and meetings with our team, I repeatedly asserted that the worship atmosphere would be an eclectic, ancient-future mix of contemporary, pop-rock, and

---

[37] Names also changed.

hymns set to classic rock. In other words, the worship at this church would not sound at all like that in most of the churches in our area. Dan and Martha sat through all those meetings, nodding in agreement. Then one afternoon I get a call from Martha, informing me that she and Dan had really been struggling with the worship style issue, and had come to the conclusion that our church just wasn't what they thought it was going to be.

One-by-one over the course of the next year, our entire core group, with the exception of my family and three others, left our church. Each had their own reasons. One young man suddenly felt "called" to attend a bigger church. Another couple left because we weren't growing as fast as they thought we should. Still another couple left a few months later because, as they put it, we were growing too fast, and as such, they weren't getting the attention, ministry, and compassion they felt they needed. The reasons given varied greatly, but the result was the same; those I thought I could count on to stick with us didn't!

The thing is, every church planter I have talked with has said that core turnover was a reality they all had to address. I'm sure there are exceptions. But remember, this book isn't about exceptions!

New Realities Post-Launch

Prior to the beginning of public worship, you are, to a large extent, working one-on-one with core members and people in the community. After launch, you suddenly become responsible for weekly worship services, facility rental agreements, building code issues, visitor follow-up, and a host of additional activities. Because of this sudden shift in ministry, your priorities will also shift, as will the way you continue to try and hold everything in balance. Because no church is the same, and because planters tend to handle things differently depending on their personalities and gifts, there really is no specifically prescribed process for making sure all the bases are covered so that you can move forward. There are, however, a few principles that deserve your attention as you move toward this stage of church planting.

Count on those who commit slowly. Simply put, people will leave you in exactly the same way that they join you. Those who responded quickly and excitedly to our invitation to church planting abandoned our efforts just as swiftly when they discovered that what we were doing just wasn't for them. Those who took their time, and were even a bit skeptical at first, were those who eventually stayed with us for the long haul.

Chad Howard[38] was the most skeptical of any potential core member who ever inquired about our church. I remember the first time he came to a meeting at our home. He asked all sorts of questions, and when he left, I had serious doubts as to whether he would ever come back. For a few months, it seemed like my prediction was accurate. Then one night, I received a call from Chad. He had been struggling for some time with whether God wanted him to do something more. Almost overnight, this

---

[38] Name not changed because he is one of my best friends and doesn't need protection.

skeptic became a staunch advocate for our church planting efforts. For the next five years, Chad, his wife Tiffani, and their children would serve faithfully. When I left the church to go to Maryland, it was Chad who gave guidance to the church. He helped lead them through a merge with an established church that would garner them property and other mature believers. Truth is, Chad had as much or more to do with our success as I did.

Chad is a glowing example of what I'm talking about. When people rush to join you, just keep in mind that they will walk out in pretty much the same way that they walk in. When people take their time, ask a lot of questions, and are honest about their skepticism, don't lose your patience with them. If these people join your team, they will most likely be in it for the long haul.

Focus on the usefulness of those who leave. If anyone in Scripture had a reason to look at the dark side of things, it was Joseph. Beaten up and sold into slavery by his own brothers, slandered by a harlot-wife because he refused to participate in her efforts to cheat on her husband, thrown into an Egyptian prison and eventually forgotten about by his former cell-mates; this guy knew what it meant to be mistreated and abused by others. He knew how it felt to have people he depended on break their word. Yet Joseph never harbored any bitterness toward these people. In fact, he testifies at the end of Genesis that each of these people were used by God to bring about something great.[39]

---

[39] Genesis 50:20

If you want to remain emotionally and spiritually healthy during your church planting experience, you must have the same attitude toward those who walk away, even those who walk away when you perceive you need them the most. As difficult as it is to see someone leave, I have to admit that each person who left us, even those who did so in anger, were of benefit to our church while they were with us. Most worked very hard to help get the church off the ground, and frankly, I'm not sure the church would even still exist today if it weren't for their service.

If possible, try to make it as positive as you can when people leave. About a year after launch, one of our young men came to me and broke the hard news; he and his wife simply could no longer handle the pressures they had placed themselves under. They needed to leave and figure out where God wanted them. I was truly heartbroken. At the same time, I had always been grateful for everything they had done. Their last Sunday with us, we recognized their service, and sent them off with a special gift. If you have to part ways with someone, do your best not to focus on their "desertion" of you. Instead, honor the service that they have given, and do it with the recognition that God has accomplished much in your church through them. Their memories of the time they spent at your church will be much sweeter, and your state of mind will be much better for doing this.

Let others "own" the church with you. I first met Elvis when he was one of my students. As a young Christian, he had a desire to reach out to those whom the church had largely rejected—people like himself. Elvis wore tattoos over most of his upper body, and his piercings made him look as though someone had thrown a tackle box at his head.

Still, his desire was to reach those who lived in the so-called "gothic" sub-culture as he did. His left arm carried the tattoos of his testimony, beginning with a picture of a bloody cross, his baptismal waters, and his gradual growth in grace. He would walk into bars and strike up conversations with people, and when they asked him about his tattoos, he would immediately roll up his left sleeve and begin telling them about Jesus.

Through his relational network, we were able to reach a lot of pierced, tattooed, black-wearing guys and gals who would likely have never entered our doors otherwise. There isn't a hole in my body that God didn't put there, meaning that I'm not at all like these people. If I had tried to reach them on my own, as I am, I doubt they would have ever given me a hearing. And why should they have? Yet they came, and they listened to the Gospel, and a few came to Jesus. This happened because I allowed Elvis to "own" part of the ministry with me.

Eventually, he helped us start a monthly concert venue called "The Fish Tank." Every month, we would see between 150 and 250 young people cram into our small building for concerts. From my perspective, the music was absolutely awful! But the people who came were attracted to the musical style, and we saw significant life change as a result. He has long since left the church, and that ministry has since been re-named "The Electric Shoe," and continues to draw people from around the community.

Allowing others to own the vision with you not only empowers them. It also takes unnecessary pressure off of you. There is no possible way for you to do everything on your own. Be willing to delegate ministry to those who are called to it and gifted for it.

Occasionally, take a break! The first year of our church plant, I took a grand total of four days vacation. My family suffered for it, and in the end, the church didn't benefit either. That was by-far the most bone-headed thing I ever did during my time as a church planter, and I did a lot of bone-headed stuff!

You will be overwhelmed at all that needs to be done. If your heart is right with God, it will break at the lostness in your community, and you will be compelled by your calling to do everything you can to break through it. You cannot accomplish anything, however, if you are dead, or divorced. I find it interesting that Jesus chose as times to "come apart" the times when it seemed like His services were needed most. Remember His example, along with the Scriptural principle that you are not above your Master.[40]

Trust God to grow His church. Our first sound system for the church was, without qualification, absolutely pathetic. Worse yet, it didn't even belong to us. Thanks to a good relationship with a worship pastor at a nearby church, we were able to borrow this

---

[40] Matthew 10: 24-31

one. Each Sunday our staff would cross their fingers, throw salt over their shoulders, knock on wood, and hope beyond hope that when we flipped the switch it would come on. We were honestly afraid that it would break while in our possession and the neighboring church would want us to pay for it. I seriously believe that thing must have run off of vacuum tubes!

After about six weeks of worship, our leadership met and decided that we could no longer continue to count on a system that every Sunday made us feel like we were rolling loaded dice. With roughly $3000.00 in the bank, we elected to purchase a sound system with the church credit card. Our only agreed-upon stipulation was that the balance on the card not exceed the amount we had in the bank.

Thankfully my brother, who at the time was running our worship program, was frugal and expeditious enough to find us a complete system online, including monitors, amplifier, and stage microphones for around $2500.00. Obviously for that price the system wasn't top of the line, but it was decent enough. Plus, it had a warranty and didn't sound like a set of broken wind chimes when we turned it on, which was more than I could say for our "borrowed" system.

Still, the fact that our young church was in debt over something like this greatly troubled me. Today when I am training church planters, I stand in front of them like a good hypocrite and warn them of the dangers of placing their needs on a credit card rather than in God's hands. During the month following that purchase, our giving and attendance stayed flat, which ratcheted up my anxieties even more.

At the time I was also working on my doctorate, and the time came to travel to the seminary for my fall seminars. The realization that I would miss a Sunday this early in the process gave me more worry still. Would anybody actually show up? Many church planters labor under this same delusion, thinking that if they "check out" for a Sunday the whole church will fall.

That Sunday afternoon I was 400 miles from my young church, nervously dialing one of my elders to find out how the services had gone, or if they had gone! To my surprise, we had the largest attendance in the history of the church to date. On top of that, someone had visited the church that morning and put a check in the offering plate, along with a note saying that they were between churches and had been holding their tithe for a few months, and had decided to give us that money. That check was made out for exactly $2500.00. When I told my wife about this, her response was simultaneously cutting, and comforting. "Don't you know" she asked, "that God had this happen while we were away just to prove to you that He doesn't need you to grow His church?"

The early days after launch will often make you feel like you are riding at top speed on an unfinished roller coaster. Just remember that this church isn't yours, it is God's, and He will take care of the growth as you are faithful to fulfill His calling. Trust Him with this new church. It was His idea anyway, wasn't it?

Taking care of a new church filled with new and "not-yet" believers requires that you get yourself ready spiritually, physically, and emotionally. Part of this preparation involves getting ready for all the challenges that await you because ultimately, the work of planting a church is the spiritual equivalent of changing diapers on a hundred babies. You have to make sure you are fit to change those diapers, which is the subject of our next chapter.

-6-

Taking Care of the Nursery

I met Gene at one of our "Fish Tank" events. Actually, the first time we met I threw him off our property. Our concert venues were totally drug and alcohol free, so when I caught him out behind our facility with a half-empty bottle of vodka, I told him it was time for him to go.

Surprisingly, a couple of weeks later he showed up at one of our worship services. Toward the end of my message, he left, highly emotional. Over the course of the next few weeks I had the opportunity to get to know Gene. The past few years had been hard on him, and he had sought comfort in liquor and drugs. By God's grace I shared Jesus with him one spring evening, and God opened his heart to the Gospel. His prayer of repentance, however, was a bit different than any I had heard before. He started by saying, "Lord, I'm a low-down, %$&#@#, dirty, $#%%*&%."

Not exactly the kind of "sinner's prayer" you see printed on the back of a Gospel tract. I admit, his language was enough for me to open an eye and raise an eyebrow. Still, this prayer was the picture of a deeply sinful man who had just become a new creature in Christ Jesus. His heart spoke truth, through words he would obviously need to learn not to use.

This chapter, and for that matter, this entire book, is written assuming that your objective is to reach into a lost world with the light of the Gospel through church planting. If your aim is simply to gather a bunch of Christians together who are just like you, you've picked up the wrong resource. However, if your heartbeat is to reach lost people and effectively teach them to be followers of Jesus, there are some important things to keep in mind.

Barking Dogs, Braying Mules, and Sinning Sinners

Though I've always enjoyed generally good health, at least once a year I end up with a sinus infection. My nose feels like it is filled with drying concrete, my chest feels contracted, and my head feels like a 10 pound bowling ball. As much as I despise going to the doctor, when these infections hit, I really have no other option.

Those visits always begin with the doctor asking me how I feel, followed by a colorful description of my symptoms (It's hard to gross out doctors, but it is fun to try!). What's interesting is that in all my years of going to the doctor, none have ever screamed at me over my symptoms. Never once has a doctor looked at me and said "Stop that coughing! Don't you know you shouldn't be

102

coughing? And that sneezing is disgusting. You need to turn away from me when you do that or you are going to get it on me! And for the love of all that is holy, you need to do something about that temperature!!!" Doctors don't scream at the symptoms of sickness. To be sure, they don't ignore them either. Ordinarily, symptoms shouldn't be there. Symptoms let you know that something isn't right. But screaming at the symptoms doesn't help. That's why doctors instead offer a diagnosis, and a cure.

Similarly, lost people will display "symptoms" of their lostness. They use foul language. They eat and drink too much. They become sexual perverts. They are greedy. They borrow more than they can afford. They lack self-control. They rebel against authority. They abort their unborn children. Most damning of all, they refuse to repent and follow Jesus. All of these behaviors, if done in a perpetual and unrepentant fashion, are symptomatic of a heart that is cold toward God and the Gospel.

Trouble is, many churches and ministries today spend an inordinate amount of time "shouting at the symptoms." Such behavior is most obvious when one observes the so-called "culture wars" in the west. Dave Burchett agrees:

> "Most of us think it is our mission as Christians to rid the world of sin. That is not going to happen. We have tried through politics and failed miserably. We have tried boycotts. When I last checked, Disney was still in business. . .We Christians have missed our calling. . .All of the cultural issues I've mentioned so far are merely

*symptoms of a bigger problem: the internal condition of
millions of people."*[41]

Our task therefore, is to accurately diagnose the real
problem, and offer the cure, realizing that sin's symptoms will
remain as long as people remain lost and separated from God.
To be sure, the church has a peripheral responsibility to engage
cultural issues in the public square from a Biblical perspective.
But ultimately, the answer to homosexuality isn't heterosexual
behavior that without Jesus, will be just as perverted. The answer
to abortion isn't ultimately a change in federal or state law. The
answer to pornography isn't putting Hefner and Flynt out of
business. The answer to all of these things is a bloody cross and
an empty tomb! Problem is, getting that message into their hearts
requires our own entrance into their lives, and in some cases,
being surrounded by their sin.

Such was our story. If you plant a church to reach lost
people, such will be your story also. Young knot-heads showed
up at church with their stripper girlfriends. Homosexual couples
showed up—together! And we let them in and welcomed them
with open arms. We did so because we realized that the only way
to speak into their lives was to share life with them.

Dogs bark. Donkeys bray. Chickens cluck. And until they
are regenerated by the power of the Holy Spirit and believe on

---

[41] Dave Burchett. *When Bad Christians Happen to Good People: Where we
have Failed Each Other and How to Reverse the Damage.* Colorado Springs:
Waterbrook Press. 128-129.

Jesus, lost people will act like lost people! Paul warns us of such behavior, and connects the sinful activity of lost people to a corrupt nature opposed to God and His law.[42] Simply put, sinful people commit sinful acts because they have sinful hearts.

Furthermore, even after they become Christians, there is often hard struggle against their former life. Honestly, if you stop and think for a minute, it's not hard to grasp this. After all, I've been a follower of Jesus for more than two decades now. By God's grace, I am not what I once was, but neither am I totally what I should be. I still have a tendency to lose my temper. As a good Baptist, I have no problem with alcohol, but battle gluttony on a regular basis, and my thought life could, from time to time, really use some work. If such is true of me, then I should expect no more from a new convert that I do from myself.

We see this in Jesus' patience with His own disciples. Too often we read the Gospels with the assumption that these twelve men became spiritual giants the moment they traded their professions to follow Him. But when you read the story slowly, you realize that a considerable amount of time passed between "Follow me, and I will make you fishers of men," and "You are the Christ, the Son of the living God."[43] In between these two moments there was personal struggle among the disciples regarding their mission, their commitment, and even their belief that Jesus was who He claimed to be! Jesus' own relationship

---

[42] Romans 1:18-32
[43] Matthew 4:19, 16:16

with His disciples illustrates well that the task of discipleship is long and messy!

Meeting them where they are

John Cramp understands this principle. Having ministered in the virtual "pagan pit" of Portland, Oregon, he tells of how he had to meet people on their own turf. "We opened our lives to them" he states, "so they could see the reality of our faith in the way we lived and related to each other. Before they could receive the message of Christ from us, they had to trust us."[44] Simply put, lost people must be reached on their own ground.

One of the things our church did every year was team up with the local recreation department to provide "Summerfest at the Planet" to the public. Rather than host this event on our own turf, we held it at a public park called Kids Planet. The Planet was one of the most popular parks in the upstate area for parents to take their children. We provided blow-up rides, free food, drawings for prizes, and a number of other activities in addition to things already going on there. We figured since Jesus called us to the people, and not the people to us, that we should go to them. For the first three years of our church we hosted this event in partnership with the city, and more than 500 people showed up each time. It gave us the opportunity to meet a lot of people on

---

[44] John Cramp. *Out of their Faces and Into Their Shoes: How to Understand Spiritually Lost People and Give them Directions to God.* Broadman and Holman Publishers, 1995, 69.

106

"neutral" ground, and open the door to opportunities to share Christ.

But there are other ways to meet people where they are. Not only must we do this from a physical standpoint, but also from an emotional and spiritual standpoint. Our church ministered to a lot of young men who carried the emotional baggage of a father who was either abusive, apathetic, or totally absent. These guys had never seen how real men take responsibility, lead in their homes and churches, and contend for the Gospel in their spheres of influence. Anyone expecting them to "grow a backbone" overnight after years of having no example would have had unrealistic expectations.

If someone is genuinely saved, we should expect to see evidence of conversion in a life that is gradually transformed by the Holy Spirit. At the same time, we shouldn't expect unbelievers to act like believers, and we shouldn't expect new believers to act like those who have walked with Jesus for years. If you want to get them to Jesus, you have to start by meeting them on their own physical, spiritual, and emotional turf.

Giving them time and room

I remember the first time I fired a shotgun. I was 10-years old, and my dad and I were in the field behind our home. My father loaded the gun and handed it to me, showing me how to shoulder the weapon, as well as how to take aim. As I took aim on a mound of dirt and wrapped my index finger around the trigger for my first shot, I felt pressure at the back of my right shoulder. I turned around to see my dad holding my back. "What are you doing," I asked in frustration. "OK then, do it on your own," he replied, and stepped back.

The thing about a 12-guage shotgun is that it packs quite a kick. I don't remember pulling the trigger. I do remember picking myself up off the ground after firing the gun! My father could have insisted on "protecting" me from that experience. Instead, his willingness to allow me some failure and embarrassment taught me a much greater lesson than his protection would have provided. Sometimes, the greater lesson comes when you recognize the futility of trying to "correct" someone and simply allowing them to fail.

Discipling new believers is a similar experience. Sometimes you must simply "back off" and give them both the time and room they need to learn in their own way. Cramp again observes that while we continue to be faithful to God's message, we can't always do God's work. "Conviction of sin," Cramp states, "is His responsibility. He works in His time. God directs the affairs of people's lives so they find themselves in an environment that heightens the awareness that their lives are not working. I continue to talk with them about Christ and explain what the Bible says about how to have a relationship with Jesus. But beyond that, I don't push."[45] Good advice!

Not only must you give those to whom you minister room to fail, but from time to time you may even have to do some self-

---

[45] Cramp. 1995, 46.

correction. During the first year of our church, our "Fish Tank" concert venue was by far the most successful of the ministries we had. With each passing month, we were looking for ways to make this venue attractive to even more people. In our enthusiasm, we invited a "black metal" band to come in and play, in hopes that we would attract more gothic-types to our venue, and subsequently, to faith in Jesus.

The guys in the band were great. As we did with every band, we reviewed the lyrics and found them Scripturally sound. Yet while standing in the back of the room listening to their performance, I realized that we had gone too far.

This realization was not due to my lack of appreciation for the genre. We hosted many bands whose musical style literally made my insides hurt. I remember standing in the back of the room next to our guy who ran the venue and saying to him "we have crossed the line." Later, I discovered the reason for the Holy Spirit's conviction. To those we were trying to reach, this particular style of music was intimately connected to self-mutilation, "cutting," and other ungodly acts against the body. Though my intentions were pure, I had not realized that this particular style of music failed what Stetzer and Elmer Towns call "the association test." This test asks the question, "does the song unnecessarily identify with things, actions, or people that are contrary to Christianity?"[46] Reggae music, for example, is not

---

[46] Elmer Towns and Ed Stetzer. *Perimeters of Light: Biblical Boundaries for the Emerging Church.* Chicago: Moody Publishing, 2004.

inherently sinful, but in certain contexts has an automatic connection with the use of drugs and therefore, should not be used as an evangelistic tool within those contexts.

Through this and other experiences, I learned that during the church planting process, you have to be vigilant in trying not to go too far. At the same time, you have to give yourself and others the room to fail from time to time. This isn't minimizing offenses when they happen. It is an admission that sometimes such offenses will happen, and people need room to mess up, repent, and try again.

Turning them into missionaries . . .early!

Carrie[47] was introduced to our church by her boyfriend, who had met her in an exotic dance club. She was a dancer, and he was a client. Carrie was saved and baptized, and subsequently got help from our church in getting out of her former profession. Not long after her conversion, she joined a women's small group led by the wife of our Associate Pastor, and sold the other ladies on finding a way to reach out to other women who were trapped in strip clubs as their only way to make a decent living.

This was definitely a new approach for our church. In honesty, I admit cringing at the thought of the media getting hold of what we were doing, and how I would be "labeled" by a few people in some of the established churches that had already made my name mud. Furthermore, we knew we had to be careful

---

[47] Name changed.

with a ministry like this. It is obvious why men might want to volunteer for this assignment, but this was, obviously, to be a 'women's only' ministry.

At the same time, I had to get past my reservations, as well as my inhibitions about what others would think. No doubt we would be accused of "enabling" ungodly lifestyles, fraternizing with sinners, and blessing perversion, when in fact we were simply stepping onto Satan's turf where Jesus expected us to be. One spring night, five of our ladies, accompanied by an elder who remained outside, went to a local gentlemen's club to take in dinner for the dancers, bouncers, bartenders, and other staff. A month later, they did it again, this time being allowed to spend some time talking with the folks who worked there. By the third month, they were going by themselves, without any of our men in the parking lot. After getting to know and respect them, the bouncers assured our guys, "no one is going to touch them while they are in here. We guarantee it!" On one occasion less than a year into this ministry, the owner shut down business for 45 minutes while our ladies paid a visit. A few people found Jesus, and eventually also found their way out. Many more were given a totally different picture of the church than they previously had. Today when the church does communion, two candles are lit on each side of the table. The holders that contain those candles were given to our ladies by the dancers.

All of this started with a former dancer who developed a heavy burden for reaching her former co-workers for Jesus.

There were plenty of reasons to pass on the opportunity, her spiritual immaturity and the risk to our church's reputation being but two of them. Ultimately, we opted to encourage this new believer in her missionary calling, and lives were changed as a result.

Another example of turning new converts into missionaries was the goth crowd that attended our church. As they found their way into our church and relationship to Jesus, they had to deal with other visitors to our church; unbelieving visitors who all but shunned them. I actually had a couple of people let me know on guest cards that they would not be back, and that I should really pray about whether I was willing to continue tolerating "people who look like that." A couple of the goths who caught on to what was happening were understandably upset and offended. My advice to them was to try and view these people the same way our church initially viewed them. They had found Jesus because someone looked past their dress and appearance, and instead of trying to make them like us, presented the Gospel so they could become like Jesus. In turn, they now had a responsibility to evangelize people, even those who didn't treat them fairly. They weren't responsible for how people reacted to them. They were however, responsible for the way they treated other people.

Over time people were won over by the goths, who looked a little strange to them, but nonetheless approached and related to them in the spirit of Christ. As a result, both the goths, and the "normal people" were able to reach and learn from each other. I

112

called this "cross-pollination discipleship." In reality, this is nothing different from what international missionaries have done for decades, but for some reason, we've been a little slow to catch on in North America.

The point however, is that new converts need to learn to share their faith early on. While they certainly need mature believers around them, the truth is that they have the distinct advantage, both of having more connections with unbelievers, and of knowing how they were brought to faith. Once people fall in love with Jesus, they should be encouraged to pass that love on to those around them.

Trusting God to bring them where they need to be

A few months prior to our move to Maryland, I took a couple of days for introspection. The church had grown, but was still small. We had helped to plant two other churches, as well as provided tangible help to a number of other church planters, but I hadn't seen the movement I had hoped I would see. As we were preparing for our final Sunday with our people, I asked Amy what exactly we had accomplished. Amy of course, hardly ever looked at what most appeal to when citing "vital statistics." Instead, she pointed to the lives God had changed during our time in South Carolina. In about 15 minutes, she spoke of half a dozen who had been saved recently, a couple of guys who were now studying for ministry, and even the change in the perception of church planting that had taken place during our nearly four-year ministry in this area.

As I listened to her speak, it became apparent to me that while we had been used by God during this time, all of the work was His. As I think back, most of the planned ministries never worked out as we thought they would. Instead, there were quite a few things that God began in our midst that we never planned. But the end result was a group of disciples congregated into a church that prior to our coming, were not congregated disciples.

When it comes to how you minister to young believers, you have to ultimately realize that this is God's work. Be faithful to Him, and to His Word, and He will do His work through you. You will be amazed at the results.

C.J. Mahanney contends that churches too often look for things to criticize in people's lives as opposed to looking for evidences of God's grace.[48] To be sure, the church exists so that fellow believers can hold each other accountable for growing in that grace, but our approach to sanctification should be governed by viewing people through the eyes of grace, not criticism and judgment.

It's interesting to note that Paul takes this approach when making necessary corrections in the church at Corinth. I don't care how badly the people in your church behave, or how immoral they are. Their sins are likely a picnic compared to the sin present in the Corinthian church. There was harsh division and an overly litigious spirit. People were treating the Lord's Supper like an opportunity to get free alcohol, and acting as though they were in

---

[48] C.J. Mahanney, in a sermon preached at Mars Hill Church in Seattle, WA.

114

a frat house instead of a church. There was sexual immorality present of the sort that appears on TV talk shows. Paul had his work cut out for him! Yet he begins his letter to this messed-up congregation by thanking God for what His grace had already done in their lives, and assuring them that through the Holy Spirit, they already had it within themselves to become all that God desired.[49]

Take care of those babes in Christ God has given you. Correct their error. Confront their heresies. Lead them toward sanctified lives. But do it all with patience, and with the confidence that the Gospel is indeed powerful enough to make them like Jesus.

---

[49] 1 Corinthians 1:4-9

-7-

About the Opposition

I've never read a more true statement about conflict than that which came from Ed Rowell. Quoting a fellow pastor, Rowell contends that the "only pastors who don't experience regular, character-building periods of conflict are either bullies who walk all over everyone, or cowards afraid to stand up for what God wants to accomplish."[50] For those whose energy has been stolen due to ministry conflict, these words, while true, are far from comforting. For the church planter who assumes that the context of a new church will somehow lessen the amount of conflict, such a statement might even be a bit surprising. What may surprise you even more are the sources from which the conflict will come. We know that the message we bring will cause us to be hated by those who reject the Gospel.[51] But when attacks and accusations

---

[50] Ed Rowell, 1997. *Leading your Church Through Conflict and Reconcilliation.* Marshall Shelley, ed. Minneapolis: Bethany House Publishers, 9.
[51] Luke 21:17

come as the result of the 'friendly fire" of fellow believers, or even from within your own heart, they are both surprising and hurtful.

Sometimes, opposition will arise from those you love the most. When we first began exploring the possibility of planting a new church in our hometown, I called the local denominational office to introduce myself to the Director. I told him I was a guy who had grown up within that area, and was saved, baptized and discipled at one of the churches that were a part of his association, and we were praying about starting a new church. Early meetings seemed to go well. But there were both theological and methodological controversies that were brewing within this area at the time, and I happened to unknowingly step right in the middle of a few of them.

In addition, there were quite a few on the Board of this association who didn't like the idea of a new church doing things in new ways. I was called to a meeting, and for two hours endured an inquisition about my theology and methodology. The most contentious moment came when one of the Board members asked "how will you expect people to dress when they come to your church?"

Remember, this meeting took place among churches in the deep south. At that time in that area there was a strong belief among many that you should dress for church in the same way that you appear in a courtroom. "When I am called before the judge," this questioner stated, "I don't go into his court in blue jeans, and I imagine God expects at least that much respect." For

118

one thing, God clothes Himself with light in such a way that no man can look upon him.[52] In light of this, I had concluded for some time that such a God would hardly be impressed by a suit and tie. Plus, as I examined the New Testament, it seemed that God was much more interested in what was in my heart than on my back when I came to worship. I did find a dress code in Scripture,[53] but it too seemed more concerned with modesty and humility, and less so with style and fashion.

So with all this in mind, I answered his question. "I will tell them," I said in response, "that they should not come to church naked." In retrospect, I admit that was a bit of a juvenile answer. Still, years later, I also believe the question was itself juvenile. He didn't seem impressed by my response, and in fact was angered.

I remained undeterred, but was surprised that such trivial concerns would cause an association's leaders to have a strong reticence toward the idea of helping a new church get started. But this experience was an emotional picnic compared to the pain I felt when I was attacked by people in my home church. I discovered that word had traveled from the associational office to the church where I was saved, baptized, and ordained regarding my plans, and that a few of the leaders were upset. I loved this church, and still do. Yet at the time, a few people in leadership there suddenly became very suspicious of me. I asked for a meeting with them, primarily because I wanted them to know I was

---

[52] Psalm 104:1-2, Exodus 33:20
[53] 1 Timothy 2:9-10, 1 Peter 3:1-5

still the guy they watched grow up there, and give them an opportunity to ask any questions they wanted. I figured my long relationship with them would override any inhibitions they may have felt about me, and that we would get clarity and understanding. I figured wrong!

I did not ask for financial support, or any other kind of tangible help. All I wanted was the approval, prayers and blessing of the church that had led me to Christ, and a few years later, laid their hands on my head and sent me out as a pastor. I was shocked to hear men that I had watched growing up, and come to respect deeply, speaking as if I were getting ready to start a cult. During our first couple of years on the field, I would hear of subsequent stinging comments that had been made about me and our church.

Conflict is never easy, but it's always hardest when it's with the people you love. Thankfully, I still keep good relationships with many of the folks at that church. Overall, it is a wonderful congregation filled with godly people and great leaders. I am happy to report that in the past several years they have grown exponentially. I am also happy that after many years, even the local association has seemed to develop a different attitude toward church planting.

Other churches were suspicious of us as well. Every time we were able to get exposure from the local press, I would get phone calls about pastors taking their sermon time to talk about our church and how evil it was because we used rock music in our worship and allowed people to enter the building wearing flip flops. On one occasion, someone tried to get me released from the University where I taught by mailing misleading information anonymously to the President about me.

Granted, most of the criticism came from the kind of churches where it's hard to discern what they are for because they spend so much time talking about what they are against. Most of the pastors were the kind who believed their church could be traced back to John the Baptist as the only "true church," believed that short hair and long faces were signs of true holiness, and believed King James was on equal par with King Jesus. But a few of the criticisms came from within my own denominational home, and they hurt. A few times, the word "liberal" got tossed around in reference to me. This was a sad surprise. Theologically, I'm a Bible-guy through and through. During my first pastorate, I was one of only a handful of pastors in an association of 19 churches who believed the Bible to be inerrant. I believe strongly in male pastoral leadership, the exclusivity of Jesus as the only way of salvation, and a literal, conscious, eternal hell for those who reject the Gospel. For these beliefs, I had garnered a few appellatives in my ministry. "Liberal" was a new one!

Truth is, if you are going to play the part of pioneer, you should expect that those who stay back on the ranch will fire a few salvos in your direction. Some of it will come from people you love and respect, and all of it will hurt. Yet in retrospect, these experiences aren't really at all different from the conflict every pastor faces in his own church. Stuart Briscoe has wisely stated that the three top qualifications for a pastor are "the mind of a scholar, the heart of a child, and the hide of a rhinoceros."[54] If you are in ministry of any kind, criticism is part of the game. Personal, hurtful, painful criticism is a reality in ministry.

Criticism and Opposition as the Plan of God

When undergoing the harshest kinds of criticism and opposition, it's hard to see God in it. Yet Jesus makes it clear that conflict, opposition, and hardship are just one more part of His calling on our lives. One of the most shocking texts in the New Testament is in Luke 22, when Jesus says to Peter, "Satan has demanded permission to sift you like wheat; but I have prayed for you that your faith may not fail; and you, when once you have turned again, strengthen your brothers."[55]

Essentially, what Jesus says to Peter is "The devil has asked me to let him make your life miserable, and I have given him that permission." Yet the reason Jesus allows such trial to enter our lives is so that our faith can be strengthened, and so that we in turn can strengthen others. In short, God is in control of the frequency and intensity of the conflict you encounter. You are in control of, and responsible for, how you react to it.

If you react in a way that honors God, you will grow in your faith, as well as strengthen others in their faith. If you react in a

---

[54] Marshall Shelley. 1994. *Well-Intentioned Dragons: Ministering to Problem People in the Church.* Minneapolis: Bethany House Publishers,, 35.
[55] Luke 22:31-32

sinful way, you may become your own worst enemy! Four months into our church planting efforts, I was still harboring hurt. The betrayal I felt from those who were opposed to what we were doing had turned into bitterness. Rather than try to view my negative experiences as opportunities for learning and spiritual growth, I did what the author of Hebrews forbids and allowed bitterness to take root in my soul.[56] This in turn created more pressure for me to "succeed," but success stopped being about bringing people to Jesus, and instead became an attempt to prove my accusers wrong. I was perpetually tired, irritable, and I am sure, more difficult to live with.

Finally one evening, my wife confronted me. "God is never going to bless our efforts here," she stated, "until you let go of all that bitterness." The Holy Spirit used her words to bring conviction on me, and over the next several weeks, I was able to get free from the chains of my own bitterness. Until that moment, there was no greater threat to the survival of our church than me!

Spiritual Attack

In a sense, all confrontation and opposition has a spiritual side to it. However, there are times when it becomes apparent that the enemy is coming directly for you. Aside from my own spiritual issue of bitterness, Satan attacked my family and my church in a number of ways. Physically, my oldest son suddenly began to suffer from seizures. Around that same time, I was

---

[56] Hebrews 12:15

diagnosed with apnea. The greatest surprise, however, came when he attacked my marriage.

Amy and I have always had a strong marriage, so we knew something wasn't right when our arguments began to escalate, and become more frequent. I was embarrassed that Satan had been able to successfully attack an area where we assumed we were strong. Yet Chuck Lawless wisely states that our strong areas are exactly what Satan is after, because he already has us in our weaknesses. "That's why they are weaknesses."[57]

All of these issues surfaced during the time we were planting the church, and I'm convinced they did not happen coincidentally. Satan loves abortion in all its forms, but loves nothing better than to kill a young church before it is fully developed. Rest assured that the enemy hates what you are trying to do, and will do everything God will allow of him to prevent your church from becoming reality. I've talked with church planters who have developed chronic illnesses, seen their children suffer from sickness, and their wives from depression. I've heard stories of awful dreams, and listened in horror to planters talk of how demonic forces attacked their children while in their beds. In the modern age, we tend to minimize or altogether ignore accounts of such events. Admittedly, there are a few "charismaniacs" out there who love to find a demon under every rock. But make no mistake, those dark spiritual forces are very,

---

[57] John Franklin and Chuck Lawless. 2001. *Spiritual Warfare: Biblical Truth for Victory.* Nashville: Broadman and Holman Publishing.

very real, and you ignore their presence, influence, power, and hostility toward your ministry at your own peril.

Attacks from the "inside"

Many of the stories you have already read describe well the kind of "inside" attacks I speak of here. People in your church will attempt to re-direct its vision. You will experience rebellion, gossip, slander and scorn. Most of your attackers will begin with well-meaning motives that eventually devolve into an attempt to defeat you "for the good of the church." Others will actively work toward your failure.

When dealing with such people, the best approach is to group them into what I call a "squeaky wheel triage."[58] Nothing is more irritating than a squeaky wheel. Whether its located on a car, a shopping cart, or a desk chair, the noise can, at times, be unbearable. But not all squeaky wheels need the same treatment. Sometimes a wheel squeaks because of a defect elsewhere. Sometimes the problem is the wheel itself, and sometimes, as annoying as the sound can be, the wheel should simply be ignored.

If the issue is a defect elsewhere, it might pay to give some attention to what the wheel is squeaking about. Sometimes even the most irritable people will say something true. If you determine that the conflict or opposition is due to a legitimate problem, then

---

[58] The "squeaky wheel" concept is adopted from Larry Osborne. 1989. *The Unity Factor: Developing a Healthy Leadership Team.* Vista, CA: Owl's Nest.

address it. Remember that the issue is not who wins the argument. The issue is a church that impacts its community the way God intends.

If the issue is the wheel itself, then it becomes necessary to confront the person directly. If they refuse to repent, you may have to dismiss them. This took place a couple of times in our church, when we were forced to confront people who were stirring discord.

Sometimes however, when there is no damage taking place to the church, you should just let a wheel squeak. In such situations, you as the leader may have to endure comments and criticisms that you'd rather not hear. If the church is not being affected by this person, and the only person they are bothering is you, then get over it for the good of everyone else, and simply ignore the complaints.

What you should never, ever do, is "grease the wheel," or give inordinate attention to complainers. Triage the issue. Based on the evaluation of your leaders, ignore the issue, face the issue head on, or fix what is genuinely wrong. Giving attention to complainers simply because they are complaining only gets you off track. Osborne states that giving too much attention to such people "sends an unspoken message to the congregation: The best way to have influence is to complain, and the louder and more often you complain, the better."[59]

---

[59] Osborne, 1989, 105.

Facing the Opposition

In church planting, opposition will come from all directions. Unbelievers will attack your message. Fellow believers will attack your methods. People on the inside will attack your character and competency. Satan will attack you, your family, and your church. With this in mind, let me suggest a few steps to take in getting ready for the opposition that is coming.

Find safe people. Simply put, find people you can trust, and to whom you can open up emotionally. Doing this with people in your church is simply dangerous, and if you aren't careful, you will talk too much to too many people and get yourself in serious trouble. What you really need are mature Christians who don't have a "dog in your fight" but who love you and have the ability to effectively minister to you and your family. If you are married, I would suggest finding an older couple who would agree to meet with you regularly for encouragement, accountability, and burden-sharing. Make sure they are able to keep things confidential, and you and your wife should agree on who these people will be. Neither spouse should use anyone as a "safe person" with whom their husband or wife is not comfortable.

Guard yourself. Temptation is a reality for anyone, and this reality becomes more intense with the added stress of a new church. As such, you should set up guards for yourself so that you don't have opportunities to stumble into sin.

One of my personal guards is that I don't meet with women alone. As a pastor, my wife, or one of my elders, would always accompany me to meet with a woman. Most of the time the type of counsel a woman needs is best given by another woman anyway, but in those cases where they had to see their pastor, I never broke this rule. In addition, if one of my female staff and I need to attend a meeting in the same place, we take separate cars. My office is charged mileage for two instead of one, but at least they know I'm not opening myself up, even to the appearance of impropriety. One of my mentors used to say "If I'm never alone with another woman, it is physically impossible to commit adultery."

Also, I try my best to never travel long distances without someone with me. In most big cities, opportunities for sin are numerous, and easily accessible, and Satan knows it. Having someone with you provides both the accountability against sin, as well as fellowship that is godly and profitable.

Since I travel a lot, my office provides me with a laptop equipped with wireless internet access. Because of the secrecy and anonymity that such equipment provides, I have to ensure that even at my computer, I'm walking in the light.[60] So, I have tracking software installed that keeps up with everywhere I have been on the internet.[61] Every week I have an accountability partner who receives an email detailing every internet site I have

---

[60] 1 John 1:7
[61] See www.covenanteyes.com

128

visited in the past seven days. In the event of temptation, the knowledge that my behavior is exposed to such light keeps me from sin.

There may be other areas in your life where temptation is strong. For example, since I don't drink and have never had a problem with alcohol, its no trouble for me to hang out in places where alcohol is served, and with people who drink it. If your past includes alcoholism, such action is extremely unwise for you. Regardless, if you know Satan is going to attack, you are foolish if you don't protect yourself by using technology, personal conviction, and the presence of other believers to protect yourself.

Learn from conflict. In looking back over my ministry, I have to admit that the times that contained the most conflict were times in which I learned the most. These experiences echo the Psalmist, who said "it is good for me that I was afflicted, that I might learn your decrees."[62] Furthermore, as much as we hate to admit, our critics really can be our best teachers. Marshall Shelley advises considering the source and spirit of any criticism to determine if their might be any educational benefit. "If a person takes the time to talk privately," Shelly says, "in person, and assures you of his love and loyalty before offering his criticism, and is willing to help with the solution, it's more likely to be a fair criticism. At least he's thought it through and is committed to solving the problem."[63] Yet even those who desire your demise will often unintentionally teach

---

[62] Psalm 119:71
[63] Shelley. 1985, 110.

you things about yourself that can be helpful. If you are able to rise above the personal offense and grow through the conflict, your worst enemies may actually provide you an advantage.

Personal conflict isn't a fun thing to contemplate. Internal struggle isn't fun to talk about. Satanic attack can seem downright scary! If you are planting an evangelistic, culture-impacting church, expect all three. If you remain faithful to God and His call through the trials, the conflict can serve as a wave you ride toward the end for which this new church was intended.

-8-

A Few Final Thoughts

If by this point you are still interested in starting a new church, it is likely that there may actually be something to this calling you perceive. It's either that, or the guys in white lab coats driving a white van should be paying you a visit real soon. Of all the things I have been privileged to do in my sixteen years of ministry, church planting was by far the most enlightening, educational, rewarding, heartbreaking, health-threatening, marriage-testing, glorious, faith-building, faith-testing, fulfilling, challenging, daunting, empowering, sweat-producing, excruciating, wonderful, God-glorifying thing I have ever done!

Through the entire experience, it is sometimes difficult to keep focused on the things that matter most. If you remember nothing else that has been said in these pages, remember the following principles. They could be the difference between a failed ministry, and hearing Jesus say "well done!"

Taking care of your relationship with Jesus

No matter how well you lead, communicate, and minister, you will never reproduce what you say. You reproduce who you are. As such, if your relationship with Christ is lacking, or not growing, you will produce a congregation of people just like you. Such is the reason why as Paul lays out a discipleship reproduction strategy for Timothy the emphasis is on finding men who are "faithful."[64] Guarding the "faith once for all delivered to the saints"[65] and passing it along is crucially important. Equipping those to whom you pass the faith to effectively pass it to others is an equally essential part of the picture. But without personal faithfulness, all you are passing along is a lot of knowledge that won't be applied and will thus result in a congregation that mirrors Paul's lamentation of those who have a form of godliness but deny its power.[66]

Sometimes in our effort to shepherd the sheep, we forget that we too need shepherding. We, like our people, are not yet where God intends for us to be, and therefore, we too must be continually developing our prayer lives, ingesting the Word of God regularly, meditating, fasting, and generally growing in grace. In addition, I would strongly recommend that you secure someone who can be a "pastor" to you. While a pastor in Kentucky, I and my family's pastor led a church just a few miles up the road from

---

[64] 2 Tim 2:2
[65] Jude 3
[66] 2 Timothy 3:5

us. But when we began to plant a church, I did not give the attention to this necessity that I should have. Even in my ministry today, I thank God for our pastor. Though my work and preaching schedule often keeps me from being at church with my family, I am able to listen to my pastor via podcast. This kind of relationship is important in ensuring that as you are helping others grow towards Jesus, you yourself are not growing away from Him.

Taking care of your family

As important to Kingdom work as church planting is, I cannot stress enough that it is far from the most important. Paul tells us clearly that anyone who will not provide for his family has denied the faith and is to be viewed by the faithful as even more reprobate than those who don't follow Jesus.[67] While most who read this text immediately and rightfully think of physical provision, it is equally important that as the head of your home, you also provide for your family spiritually and emotionally. Simply put, your top priority above all else, including church planting, is your wife and children.

I love what I do. Honestly, there are days when it is hard to believe a paycheck comes with this job. I love working with pastors and churches. I love helping to equip churches to reproduce themselves by winning disciples, planting churches, and reaching their communities and the world with the Gospel. But what I love even more is the fact that God has given me a wife and two sons.

---

[67] 1 Timothy 5:8

As I write these words, I'm in the air somewhere between Phoenix Arizona and my home. God willing, in about an hour I'll be touching down at the Baltimore-Washington International Airport. Less than an hour after touchdown, I'll be walking through the front door of my home. Within seconds of hearing the door open, my two-year-old will come barreling out of his room, down the hall and around the corner, probably with sticky hands and drool all over his face from eating a sucker. He will "attack" his dad by grabbing me around my legs. About the time I pick him up, my seven-year-old, will have heard me come in and will run down the hall from his room, and I will hear "Daddy!" as both boys pile on top of me for an awesome wrestling match.

At some point I will look up from the living room floor where my two boys have me pinned and see my beautiful bride of fourteen years. (In case you can't tell, I've been away for a few days and this plane can't land soon enough!) She and I will give each other a long embrace, and she will give me that smile that always seems to make me go weak; the smile that says with one look, "I love you so much, and I'm so glad you are home." God's grace has allowed me to be a part of some incredible ministry moments, but none of them compare to the satisfaction I feel when I think about my family. For that reason, I realize that "ministry" begins in my own home, and I would gladly leave vocational ministry tomorrow if I sensed it to be the best thing for my wife and boys.

Unfortunately, I haven't always felt this way, and too many planters operate the way I did; with a willingness to sacrifice the family for the ministry. Some don't raise enough money to support their family through church planting, and instead of going bi-vocational, force their wives to get a job and leave the important role of raising the children to a stranger in a daycare center. Some don't give their family the time and attention they need and deserve from their husband and/or dad. Don't make this crucial error. Your church may grow to be the "exception," but if you let your family down in the process, you are a colossal failure. Conversely, if the church tanks, but you continue to be the godly husband and father that Scripture commands, then when you stand before Jesus, He will let everyone know you have done your job well, and that is all that matters in the end.[68]

Operating from character, not just competency

If God has gifted you with the skills necessary to start a church, it is likely you have some incredible talents that will shine during the process. Perhaps your skills as a visionary are such that people literally experience the future when you speak of it. Maybe your abilities to organize, delegate, and execute strategy allow people to quickly find their place and fulfill their calling in a new church. Maybe you have oratory skills that hold people spellbound as you expound on God's Word. Thank God for such talents, but don't ever, ever depend on them!

---

[68] Matthew 10:26

Early in the life of our church, there was so much to be done that I would allow my sermon preparation time to be stolen away by what should have been lesser priorities. As a result, I spent a few Sundays leaning into my preaching gift instead of taking the time necessary in God's Word. In short, I cheated my people, and if you lean into your gifts to compensate for effort you should be giving, you will do the same thing. After a few weeks, I was gently rebuked by a friend who reminded me that nothing was more important than adequately preparing to feed my people God's Word.

The gifts God has given you can be used for good or ill. How your gifts are used depends to a large extent on whether you lean into Jesus, or your skills, when the pressure is on. Just remember that competencies will only carry you so far. Character and calling last beyond your time in ministry, as well as vindicate its legitimacy.

Expanding in stages

Somehow I really thought it was possible, with 13 faithful adults in our core group, to have several comprehensive ministries functioning adequately from day one. Because my picture of the "end game" included a full, age-graded children's program, a full band, and at least four small groups from the start, I simply lost touch with reality in my efforts to make this happen early. The result early in our plant was that people were burned out, ministries were started with insufficient resources, and because we were "spread too thin," we did nothing well.

136

After a few months (and sadly, a few burned out people), my brain finally caught up with my imagination and we cut back to ministries that, for our size, were more manageable. Worship music included a guitarist and keyboard player, who were sometimes helped out by backup tracks. "Children's Ministry" included a nursery for bed babies and a Sunday School for children 2-5 that ran simultaneous with the worship service. Two small groups formed the base of our discipleship and fellowship plans.

After some time, we saw all of these areas begin to expand. When I left the church to go to Maryland, we had a full worship band, six small groups, our "Fish Tank" concert venue, two daughter churches, and an international partnership with Central America. But what I learned the hard way is that if you try from the beginning to be everything for everybody, you end up doing nothing well for anybody.

The temptation of starting things before the right time, deep down, comes primarily from pride. Many church planters, including yours truly, want to be recognized for their accomplishments. I'll talk about ego in a moment, but for now I'll simply say that if you want to accomplish anything of genuine and lasting value, you need to have the patience to watch things grow slowly, and the perseverance to expand in stages. Don't do too much at once. You, your people, and the community you are trying to reach will all suffer for it.

Having a mindset for reproduction

Simply put, you need to view the planting of daughter churches as a priority equal to personal evangelism, Biblical preaching, and church growth. Develop an attitude within yourself and your people that assumes your church to be a failure if it doesn't reproduce!

At the same time, plan wisely for such activity. While a super-majority of churches in North America wait too long, or simply never start another church, it is also possible to "parent" a church too early. In retrospect, our first "daughter" was conceived too early. Our denomination asked us to parent this new church while we were still "adolescents" ourselves, and as a result, both we and the church we planted suffered. To be sure, I don't blame the denomination at all for this. The fact is that I should have known and recognized the premature nature of such a proposal.

The second time, however, we were much more ready to assume the responsibility. I've had planters ask me before how to know when it is time to reproduce. While that question will be answered differently by different churches, I think there are three general measurements that can help one gauge whether it is truly time to birth a baby.

First of all, there will be a need that is made obvious to the church leadership. Today in North America, "need" can be established by merely throwing a dart at a US map. In an environment where more than 3500 churches die every year, the need for new churches is everywhere. Still, God hasn't called

138

your church to plant everywhere, meaning that part of discerning the right time to reproduce will include an unusual burden for a particular area where a church is needed.

Second, you will notice that God is raising leaders for the task. Sometimes the leader of the new church will rise up from within your own congregation. In our case, both church planters came from outside our church. Nevertheless, keep an eye out for potential leaders in whom Jesus is working.

Finally, there will usually be other partners who will vindicate the burden you have. In our case, the passion of our leadership for reproduction was strengthened by a qualified and available planter, people who wanted to join that planter, and supportive denominational personnel. In the end, God's call for your church to plant in a particular location will generally be accompanied by others who share that burden.

Take your time when considering how you will parent a new church. Make sure God is truly telling you that it is time to plant a new church. Make sure others in your church, and outside your church, also sense that it is time. At the same time, keep the vision of church planting on the agenda, and burned into your heart.

Checking your ego at the door

Six months after our launch, I was at the point at which almost every church planter arrives; the point where you start to wonder if your church is even going to survive. While many books on the subject suggest fast growth within the first year, the fact is

139

that many church planters will spend the first twelve months after launch feeling as though they are trying to roller skate across wet cement. In most cases, things simply move much more slowly than you think they will.

Of course, I didn't realize this, and found myself in a panic because our worship attendance was still in the 30s. Emotionally, I was a mess, thinking I was on the verge of certain failure. I called a fellow pastor who had started a church a few years before me to get advice. In my frustration and fear, I even treated his secretary horribly over the phone. Thankfully, I was given the chance to apologize for my behavior, and she graciously forgave me.

When I finally sat down with my friend, he asked me point blank what I was so worried about. "All my life," I responded, "I have never, ever failed at anything I have tried to do, and I am scared to death of being a failure." He was sympathetic, while simultaneously reminding me that my attitude was caused by the same rotten pride that got Satan kicked out of heaven and Adam kicked out of the garden. It was a sobering, but necessary reminder.

The moral of this story is simple; church planting, like any other ministry, isn't about you. John Piper reminds us of this fact when he states that we can "mark it down: God will hide from you much of your fruit. You will see enough to be assured of His blessing, but not so much as to think you could live without it. For

God aims to exalt Himself, not the preacher, in this affair of preaching."[69]

Sadly, too many men enter ministry looking for approval, praise, and personal affirmation. If this describes you, please do us all a favor and don't plant a church, or repent before you do. If you depend on a new church to inflate your ego, you will never lead your people toward humility, and God will not be honored by your ministry.

Keeping your focus on the mission

It was a beautiful spring Sunday afternoon, and while I should have been outside somewhere with my family, instead I was sulking over a low-attendance, and an even lower offering. The phone rang later that afternoon and I picked it up--with fleeting thoughts of quitting ministry and going to truck driving school--to find Kim on the other end of the line.

Kim was an absolute sweetheart. She had been dating a guy who was attending our church, and for the past several weeks had been hanging out with some of our people and exploring what it meant to have a relationship with Jesus. I had no idea her search was about to end!

During our conversation, Kim told me that my sermons over the past few weeks had "deeply troubled" her. Some nights she even had trouble sleeping, and the thought that she might actually be at odds with her Creator had created an anxiety within

---

[69] John Piper. *The Supremacy of God in Preaching.* Grand Rapids: Baker Book House, 2004. 23.

her that she couldn't get rid of. An hour later, I and an elder met her at the church. Before that day ended, Kim asked Jesus to forgive her of her sins, and became a child of God.

Sitting home that evening, I suddenly realized that all the things I had been pouting about earlier in the day didn't matter anymore. And those things won't matter when you keep your focus where it belongs; on changed lives. The point of church planting isn't having a healthy bottom-line, a large organization, or even a sizeable congregation that attracts the attention of the city. While all these things are commendable, the point is that people are changed by the Gospel. Don't ask yourself how big your church is. Ask yourself how many lives have been transformed by Jesus. It really is the mission that matters!

I really hope this book is helpful to your church planting efforts. You will see God do absolutely incredible things. There is truly no richer reward on earth than watching God use your young church to save people who would likely not come to Christ in any other way. Nevertheless, this line of work isn't for the faint of heart. It's hard, slow, demanding, and taxing on the body, mind, and soul. But it's encouraging to know that in the end, Jesus will take the fruit He brings to bear from your church, and add it to that grand, multi-ethnic, universal body of believers whom Revelation tells us is so large that it cannot be counted. Be grateful for the opportunity to play a part in this greatest of all plans.

-Epilogue-

It was March 12, 1971, and Jack Lengyel had just been installed to the most unenviable position in college football. After four years as head coach at the College of Wooster in Ohio, Lengyel was hired as the new head coach at Marshall University. Problem was, he was a coach without a team!

On November 14 of the previous year, 37 football players for the Marshall Thundering Herd were on board Southern Airways flight 932 when it crashed less than 2000 yards from its intended runway in Ceredo West Virginia. Deemed "unsurvivable" by the National Transportation and Safety Board upon investigation, the crash killed all 75 aboard, including the flight crew, the players, eight coaches, and 25 boosters. The University, as well as the entire town of Huntington, West Virginia, was devastated.

To say that Lengyel had signed up for a tough job would be the understatement of the century. His task was to rebuild a football team that was essentially non-existent, amidst opposition both internal and external. With only three veteran players, he had to petition the NCAA to allow his team to play freshmen. Some supporters of the University were extremely upset, and many felt it was inappropriate, and dishonoring to those who had died in the plane crash, to begin trying to rebuild the team only one season later. After a crushing first-game loss to Morehead State, many more began to wonder whether the rush to rebuild did little more than insult the memory of the 1970 team that had perished.

Still, Lengyel's vision was to rebuild the Marshall football program into something great. At the same time, he was realistic enough to realize that such greatness would not likely be attained in a single season. Most likely, the rebuilding effort would not be complete until long after his tenure at Marshall had ended. "If it's a miracle you are looking for," Lengyel told the local press at his formal installation, "then you will all end up disappointed, and I will end up out of a job." Sure enough, Marshall posted a record of 2-8 in 1971, bringing Lengyel's short-term predictions to pass. By the time Lengyel left the Marshall program in 1974, he had compiled a combined record of 9-33 as Marshall's head coach.

But Lengyel's success can't be defined by his win-loss record. It must be viewed through his attempts at turnaround, and the embodiment of those attempts seen in a single game against Xavier College. In the second game of the 1971 season, Lengyel led his young, inexperienced Thundering Herd to a 15-13 victory over their heavily favored rivals. This single win gave hope to the

144

team, the school, and the community that they could, and would, recover.

For a while, it looked as if things would never get better. Throughout the 1970s, Marshall lost more football games than any other college team in the nation. But in 1984, the turnaround finally became apparent. Between 1984 and 2004 the Thundering Herd enjoyed 21 straight winning seasons, including two Division 1-AA National Championships in 1992 and 1996. Now a Division 1-A school, Marshall has played in seven bowl games in the last nine seasons. Across the NCAA, Marshall is recognized as a force to be reckoned with. More than three decades ago, Jack Lengyel helped the team begin this journey to greatness, but never saw any of it as Marshall's head coach.

This story has since been made into a film entitled "We are Marshall," released in 2006. Every time I think of this fascinating story, I'm reminded that greatness takes time, most things that really matter aren't accomplished in a couple of years, and lasting success is most often preceded by lots of hard work, disappointment, and even short-term failure. In other words, when I think of this story, I think about church planting!

In Revelation 7, John gives us a vision of the church as it one day will be. It is so large that mathematics fails at measuring its size. It is so diverse that every language ever known to man will be spoken in praise to God. It is so multi-national that no ethno-linguistic people group who has ever lived will be left out. It is so pure that all are robed in white; so worshipful that all are waving their palm branches; so radically God-centered that their worship of the Lamb does not cease for all eternity.[70]

Seeing this picture I have to admit, my church plant didn't look anything like this group! I'm guessing yours won't either. As Jack Lengyel led the Thundering Herd, you and I are helping lead churches to greatness. A few of us will actually see small glimmers of such greatness as our churches grow into the hundreds, or maybe even into the thousands. Most of us will see nothing like this. In fact, chances are you will be within the more than 99 percent of church planters whose congregation never gets mentioned alongside Saddleback, Mars Hill, Willow Creek, Flamingo Road, or Mosaic.

Even if you are blessed to be among the less than 1 percent who grow to prominence, you still must realize that your church is merely a small microcosm of the greater Kingdom of God and the immeasurable universal church. Your significance, and your success, cannot be defined within the short time-span of this life, which Scripture tells us lasts comparatively as long as the midst coming from your mouth in winter.[71]

But smallness does not equal insignificance. Not by a long shot! You must have realistic expectations, but you must also see those expectations in light of the coming King and His Kingdom. Jesus saves people in the real world. Lives are changed, communities are impacted in a positive way, and churches are

---

[70] Revelation 7:9-12
[71] James 4:14

146

planted in the real world. God did, and still does remarkable things through churches of all sizes, and He will do remarkable things through your efforts as well. I pray that as you answer His call to plant, you will be reasonable concerning your own abilities, while expecting Jesus to do the unfathomable in His own time with your efforts. And yes, it is indeed worth the effort!

Selected Bibliography

Akin, Daniel L., ed. 2007. *A Theology for the Church.* Nashville: Broadman and Holman.

Anthony, Michael J. 1997. *The Effective Church Board.* Eugene, OR: Wipf and Stock Publishers.

Dave Burchett. 2002. *When Bad Christians Happen to Good People: Where we have Failed Each Other and How to Reverse the Damage.* Colorado Springs: Waterbrook Press.

Carter, Les and Jim Underwood. 1998. *The Significance Principle: The Secret Behind High Performance People and Organizations.* Nashville: Broadman and Holman.

Neil Cole. 1999. *Cultivating a Life for God: Multiplying Disciples Through Life Transformation Groups.* Carol Stream, IL: ChurchSmart Resources.

Cramp, John. 1995. *Out of Their Faces and Into Their Shoes: How to Understand Spiritually Lost People and Give Them Directions to God.* Nashville: Broadman and Holman.

Driscoll, Mark. 2004. *The Radical Reformission: Reaching Out without Selling Out.* Grand Rapids: Zondervan.

Engle, Paul E. and Steven Cowan, eds. 2004. *Who Runs the Church? 4 Views on Church Government.* Grand Rapids: Zondervan.

Franklin, John and Chuck Lawless. 2001. *Spiritual Warfare: Biblical Truth for Victory.* Nashville: Broadman and Holman

Lewis, Robert. 2000. *The Church of Irresistible Influence.* Grand Rapids: Zondervan.

Malphurs, Aubrey. 1998. *Planting Growing Churches for the 21st Century.* Grand Rapids: Baker Book House.

David Murrow. 2005. *Why Men Hate Going to Church.* Nashville: Thomas Nelson Publishers.

Osborne, Larry W. *The Unity Factor: Developing a Healthy Church Leadership Team.* Vista, CA: Owl's Nest.

Piper, John. 2004. *The Supremacy of God in Preaching.* Grand Rapids: Baker Book House.

Rainer, Thom and Eric Geiger. 2006. *Simple Church: Returning to God's Process for Making Disciples.* Nashville: Broadman and Holman.

Marshall Shelley. 1994. *Well-Intentioned Dragons: Ministering to Problem People in the Church.* Minneapolis: Bethany House Publishers.

Glenn Smith. 2007. *Improving the Health and Survivability of New Churches: State of Church Planting USA.* Leadership Network. [database online]; available from www.leadnet.org; Internet

Stanley, Andy. 1999. *Visioneering: God's Blueprint for Developing and Maintaining Personal Vision.* Sisters, OR: Multnomah Publishers.

Stanley, Andy and Ed. Young. 2002. *Can We Do That? 24 Innovative Practices that will Change the Way you do Church.* USA: Howard Publishing

Stanley, Andy, Reggie Joiner and Lane Jones. 2004. *7 Practices of Effective Ministry.* Sisters, OR: Multnomah Publishers.

Stetzer, Ed. 2003. *An Analysis of the Church Planting Process and Other Selected Factors on the Attendance of SBC Church Plants.* Alpharetta, GA: The North American Mission Board.

Towns, Elmer and Ed Stetzer. 2004. *Perimeters of Light: Biblical Boundaries for the Emerging Church.* Chicago: Moody Press.

Warren, Rick. 1995. *The Purpose-Driven Church: Growth Without Compromising your Message and Mission.* Grand Rapids: Zondervan.

White, James Emery. 1997. *Rethinking the Church: A Challenge to Creative Redesign in an Age of Transition.* Grand Rapids: Baker Book House.

About the Author

Dr. Joel Rainey is Director of Mid-Maryland Baptist Association, a network of more than 50 evangelical churches in the Baltimore-Washington D.C. area. He has been a pastor in South Carolina, Kentucky, and Maryland, and has been involved in planting more than 30 churches in the United States. He has also served as a Missions professor at both college and seminary levels. He received a B.A. from North Greenville University, and received both the M.Div. and Ed.D. from The Southern Baptist Theological Seminary in Louisville, Kentucky.

He lives in central Maryland with his wife Amy and their two children, where he enjoys spending time with his family, and riding his Harley.

CPSIA information can be obtained at www.ICGtesting.com
259989BV00004B/76/P

9 780979 805325